CHANGE WITHOUT STRESS FOR BUSINESS SUCCESS

How to Implement Change with Enthusiasm

Henry C. Ekstein, Ph.D.

Foreword by

James Watson, Vice President, ADP

Management Perceptions
Teaneck, New Jersey
Phone: (201) 833-8041

http://www.managementperceptions.com

Copyright © 2005 Henry C. Ekstein, Ph.D.

All rights reserved. No part of this book may be reproduced in any way, or by any means, without permission in writing by the author, except in case of brief quotations embodied in reviews and articles.

In memory of my beloved parents, who
taught me the value of education

Table of Contents

Foreword *8*

Introduction *12*

Chapter 1. Twelve Roses *17*

Chapter 2. The Pairing of Options Principle *32*

Chapter 3. The Bull's Eye Principle *40*

Chapter 4. Keep It Simple *67*

Chapter 5. Evaluation of Employees Made Simple *79*

Chapter 6. The Sisyphus Principle *86*

Chapter 7. The Matchmaker's Principle *94*

Chapter 8. The "Hook in the Wall" Principle *103*

Chapter 9. A Matter of Faith *113*

Chapter 10. The Sexton's Principle *124*

Chapter 11. Changing the President's Image *140*

Chapter 12. Information Systems Pitfalls *146*

Chapter 13. The Power of Encouragement *151*

Chapter 14. Penny-wise, Dollar-foolish *160*

Chapter 15. Teaching Old Dogs New Tricks *168*

Chapter 16. Persistence Pays *177*

Chapter 17. The "Slotting" Principle *186*

Chapter 18. The Big Rocks Principle *192*

Dedication

This book is dedicated to all my past employers. To those who hired me, to those who promoted me, and above all, to those who fired me, because were it not for their valiant efforts, I would not have achieved the success I enjoy today.

Foreword

by
James Watson

When Henry called me recently and asked me if I would be willing to write the foreword for a book that he was authoring, my first reaction was one of surprise. Henry and I had not talked for many years. I was surprised, but also deeply moved, that I could do something for a man whose ideas have brought profound change to the way in which I live.

My business dealings with Henry began some years ago when he gave several briefings at ADP, the company I work for, about how to handle and manage change and how to look at things from different perspectives. I was so impressed with what he had to say that I asked Henry to give some additional briefings to the organizations over which I had responsibilities. I was not only impressed with his message but with the way he presented his ideas, instantly drawing his audience into active participation. His message was always clear, easily understood and easily applied. His style was always entertaining, which helped to keep our attention focused, and studded with practical examples of how to apply his various principles. As usual Henry again did an outstanding job in presenting these ideas to my organization, so much so that I felt compelled to express my appreciation and gratitude in a letter to the editor of <u>Success</u> magazine, which published an article about Henry's methods. In the end of this letter I wrote, "Perhaps Oliver Wendell Holmes best expressed my experience with Dr. Ekstein when he said 'Man's mind, once stretched by a new idea, never regains it's original dimensions.'" I don't often write these types of letters but it was probably this letter that had caused Henry to call me about writing this foreword.

What Henry did not know when he called me, however, was how our meeting and his management briefing had impacted my own life and career. It wasn't until our conversation on the phone, that Henry realized how much of his "lessons" I still remembered after so many years and how much I still used them to this day. I use and share many of Henry's lessons and ideas with others in order to help them see things from a different point of view, to try and help myself and others solve problems that for a time might seem insolvable. Putting things into the right perspective is not always easy, however, some of Henry's "principles" and stories do help by giving you a framework for thinking clearly, and helping you discover new options. Recognizing what can and can't be done about a problem is often the difference between working towards a feasible solution and chasing an illusive answer. I learned from Henry, that rather than trying to deal with a problem try to eliminate it by applying the "Sexton's principle." Henry's ideas are powerful and applying them will help you make better decisions in your business and personal life.

Each of us meets many different people in the course of our life, socially and in business. People come and go. A few, like Henry, make a lasting impression. While undoubtedly Henry is an extremely intelligent man, his message is not complicated or difficult to understand. His "principles" are easy to apply. Each one is simple and straightforward. It is practical and it can make a difference. He has a gift for making you think about familiar things in new ways in order for you to appreciate that changing your perspective about things can, in fact, change your life. Henry is a storyteller. He takes real life situations that have occurred to him or to people he knows and relates them to his "lessons" or "principles". He will, on occasion, throw in a proverb or two to make a point. His message is both entertaining and timeless. It is valid today and it will be equally valid a hundred years from now.

Finding ways to make sense of and deal with change is an integral part of life. Each year the rate and significance of those changes just accelerates. This year there will be more change than last year but less than the next year, and so on. Change often brings stress but, like dealing with change, dealing with stress is also part of life. Therefore, anything that helps us to better understand change and how to cope with it will ultimately help us to better manage stress, which, in turn, will help us lead happier and more productive lives.

Many organizations have recently embraced the idea that diversity is not only a social requirement but also a real asset. People of different ages, sexes, and cultures do not all think alike and thanks to these differences our perspectives are expanded, our minds broadened, which helps us cope with change. While there are many books dealing with the subject of change I think you will find this book uniquely different. For example, to a client whom a bank denied a loan he needed for buying machinery, Henry said, "Why did you go to the bank for a loan? I will help you pick up money from your floor." In other words, he'll show you how to grow with what you already have, because Henry believes that even in best run companies there is plenty of waste that can be eliminated and the savings can be put to better use.

Henry's book and its message couldn't come at better time.

The above represents my views as an individual, not as a representative of my company.

James Watson
Vice President, ADP

Introduction

Whenever I give a management briefing, the participants ask me, "Why don't you write a book?" After hearing this question so many times, I realized that I should write a book. So here it is.

The book shows how human nature, with its inherent weaknesses and frailties, affects our decision-making and our actions. You will also learn from this book that there are good reasons for you to free yourself of your fears and worries, which often prevent you from making decisions and taking action. Among others, you will also learn:

- How to choose the best of many options
- What to do and what not to do, when you are laid off
- How to avoid being put down by others
- How to generate and implement new ideas,
- How to develop enthusiasm instead of resentment to change in business and personal life
- How to develop the abilities of managers and employees and discover new management talent in your workforce
- How to determine if, when and how your operation can best use outside help

- Why solutions are sometimes based on factors that have nothing to do with the problem at hand and how to prevent this from happening
- How to get the best from your managers, supervisors and employees

The book contains many of my management and management consulting theories as well as some personal experiences. It also contains studies of cases I encountered in my work. Many of these case studies are the result of common efforts of managers and employees of my clients, who worked with me. These projects saved my clients millions of dollars, and improved the managerial skills of everyone involved helping many managers be promoted, some of them becoming presidents and vice presidents of their companies. I've also included some short stories I found to be a source of wisdom useful for meeting challenges in life. Learning from these case studies and stories may help you make better decisions at work and in your personal life.

Some chapters of this book include material that I introduced in national and trade magazines. Other chapters contain material that I presented at management briefings for various companies, at seminars at Harvard University and at the "Inc. Conference on Growing the Company."

Due to considerations of confidentiality, I have changed the names of companies their managers and their titles to protect their identities, except in cases where the company and executives agreed to be mentioned by name. If despite the fictitious names of managers and companies you still think that you know who they are, this is because the situations we discuss in the book are real and are prevalent in many companies, perhaps even in yours.

The book contains what I call "principles." These are common sense insights derived from case studies and stories that have wide applications for solving a broad range of problems. Some of the principles show how to solve problems and some show dangerous pitfalls to avoid. You may find them useful in projects or problem-solving you undertake in the future. They deal primarily with common preconceptions and human frailties that prevent us from seeing problems objectively and sometimes cause us to develop solutions that are worse than the problems they purport to solve.

Should you encounter a problem that you have solved by applying one of these "principles" or a pitfall that you have avoided please contact me. It will help me in the development of new case studies for my future management briefings. I can be reached in the U.S. at (201) 833-8041.

I would also like to point out that the chapter "Twelve Roses" was added because some of my friends and business associates were either laid-off, or were afraid that they would be laid-off in the near future. I had many discussions with them, trying to ease their fears. Being laid-off is nearly always an unpleasant experience, even if you have a contract ensuring high severance pay. I, therefore, thought that including the chapter "Twelve Roses" would be helpful to readers who fell on hard times, or are concerned that they may soon.

Do not think that "Twelve Roses" is only relevant in good times. It is true that finding a job in bad times is more difficult than finding one in good times. It is also true though, that if you look hard you can find a job or start a business even during bad times. The rule is that you must look for a job or start a business when you are ready, and not when times are good. I know a man who wanted to open a business but was waiting for times to get better. This fellow became gray before he could decide that times were good enough. Do not let this happen to you.

Thanks are due to James Watson of ADP for writing the foreword. I found the managers of ADP very open-minded, whether I gave a management briefing or worked on a project. Their open-minded attitude helped me refine some of the ideas presented in this book. Thanks are also due to Mark S. Newman Chairman, President and CEO of DRS Technologies, Inc., and to Chuck Feingold, President and CEO of Valor, Inc., who agreed to the use of their names and their company names in case studies; to William H. Swanson,

Chairman and CEO of Raytheon Company, for offering the use of his refreshing booklet[*] that I quoted in various chapters and for reviewing the manuscript and making important comments which helped me improve the text; to George Buckley, Chairman and CEO of Brunswick Corporation, who inspired me to write two chapters of this book; to Varda Brief for drawing some of the cartoons; to Dr. Ilana Michelson for her insightful suggestions; to Ralf Hettler for designing the jacket; and to Benjamin S. Michelson, who edited the book, added to it his own valuable ideas, and displayed great patience with my many changes to the manuscript.

Last, but not least, I wish to thank my clients, their managers and employees who encouraged me to write this book. I also wish to thank all those who worked with me on the various projects and thus helped develop the case studies contained in this book. Without their input, this book would not have been possible.

---

[*] William H. Swanson, *Swanson's Unwritten Rules of Management*, Raytheon Company, 2004.

Chapter 1

Twelve Roses

> Keep away from people who try to belittle your ambitions. Small people always do that, but the really great make you feel that you, too, can become great.
>
> — *Mark Twain*

The day started like any other. The telephones were ringing, the fax machine was making its usual noises and my secretary had just finished proofreading a draft of a report I had written. John, the production manager, brought himself a cup of coffee from the small kitchen. He sat in the room across the hall from my office, poring over inventory reports with deep concentration. Holding a coffee cup in his right hand, he carefully reviewed the availability of parts for tomorrow's production schedule. The door to his office was open as was mine, so that each of us could see what the other one was doing.

At eleven o'clock, John asked my secretary, Susan, "Did they distribute the checks yet?"

"Not yet," answered Susan.

At that time, I was a vice president of a Fortune 500 high-tech division. I had hired John some years ago as an assistant production manager and had promoted him later to production manager. After a number of years, John reported to another executive, Robert, who was an excellent, very demanding manager and a very decent man. He was not sure that John was the right man to handle the job in a fast growing company and was planning to transfer him to a less demanding position.

As fate may have it, if you stay too long in a company you begin to be taken for granted. You become like a fixture or a piece of furniture, which everyone expects to see forever but no one appreciates. If you stay even longer, you will eventually report to someone who will not like your performance or personality. He will either demote you or make your life so miserable, that you will want to leave on your own. He might even let you go outright, depending on the culture of your organization.

This can happen to you even if you have the ability, the skills and the will to perform your job. Most probably, more people are laid-off for personal or political reasons than for lack of ability.

Robert was not sure what to do with John until this fateful payday. On this day, they distributed the checks at 11:40. John did not wait for lunchtime, but went to the bank to deposit his check, because he had promised his wife to take her out for lunch. When John left, the time was 11:40 AM. At 11:50

Robert needed John urgently and was told by his assistant that John had left for lunch ten minutes ago.

After depositing the check at the bank, John met his wife at a nearby diner for lunch. When John came back, it was twenty minutes past one.

Robert did not lose any time and summoned John to his office. "Do you know what the working hours are in this company?" He asked John.

"What do you mean?"

"I mean when does lunch start and when does it end?"

John did not like where this conversation was leading.

Robert continued, "You certainly don't seem to know. I was in your office at ten minutes to twelve, I needed you urgently and your people told me that you left for lunch. Lunch starts at twelve o'clock. This is unacceptable behavior, especially for a manager."

"But you know that I often stay extra hours to make sure that all my work is done. On balance I am putting in more hours than I am required." answered John in despair.

"One thing has nothing to do with the other. You are setting a bad example for your subordinates. Imagine everyone going to lunch when they please, and returning when they please. Where would we be?"

"But other managers also take the liberty of occasionally leaving earlier for lunch."

"Even if other managers leave early, it is still wrong. Besides, I think that your job is too big for you. Maybe we should start looking for something more suitable to your abilities."

Perhaps John said some improper words to Robert in the heat of the discussion, because at the end Robert said to John, "You're fired!"

"But you have no reason to fire me!" said John.

This is what John related to me, when he came to my office ten minutes later. He had tears in his eyes.

"I am going to sue Robert and the company. I want to know why they're firing me."

"Don't let your emotions get the best of you. You must keep your cool and act rationally", I said to John.

"What difference does it make to you why you are fired?" I said to him. "How will this help you? You will be much better off leaving on good terms. You may need the company for recommendations or perhaps even a job in the future. Leaving on bad terms can only hurt you."

"I want to know why. It is probably age discrimination. I'm nearly thirty-eight-years old and they probably plan to hire someone in his early twenties for half the money. It is not that I am earning too much. With four children I can barely make ends meet on my salary. Do you know how much it costs to buy underwear for four children? I am driving a twelve-year-old car because I cannot afford to buy a new one. Now, I will not even have this meager salary. For eight years, I was doing a good job. Now suddenly I'm no good. I am going to sue them and get my job back."

I tried to talk John out of suing the company. "They can afford to spend more on lawyers than you. You are probably going to lose. If you force them to think why they let you go, they will find good reasons. They will convince both the judge and themselves that you are not a good man, that you have made terrible mistakes, and that they had no choice but to let you go. Will you be better off that way? If you ask me, they have done you a big favor. Why work for a boss that does not like you when you can pick one who will be happy to have you on his team? As William Swanson of Raytheon said, 'You cannot pick your family but you can pick your boss.' Besides, you yourself told me, that you could barely support your family on your present salary. Here is your opportunity to get a better boss and a better job with better pay. You should not sue them; you should really send them a dozen roses with a thank you note."

"You are making fun of me. It is easy for you to say so, because you have a good and secure job". When John said it, he was almost crying. I tried to pacify him.

"John, You yourself know best how capable and hard-working you are. Do not let anyone tell you otherwise. No one can make you look bad unless you let him, unless you agree with him. If you do not agree with him, if you do not think that you are a poor manager, what do you care what someone thinks? He can think whatever he wants. It does not matter, as long as you believe that you are a good man and a capable executive. In fact, if you know how good you are, it means the opposite, since whoever thinks you are not a good manager is simply a poor judge of people and, therefore, cannot be a good manager himself. On the other hand, if you agree with your boss that you are not a good manager, you give him a powerful weapon. You agree that he can be your judge and tell you whether you are good or not. Why would you want to give him such power over you?"

"Henry, what you are saying makes sense, but you are forgetting that he just fired me. How will I feed my family now?"

"John, you must look at the larger picture to see things from the proper perspective. Let me ask you something. Do you know how many people live in the United States? There are more than two hundred fifty million. How many work in our company, eight hundred? This leaves close to two hundred fifty million people who do not have a job here. Do they all starve from hunger? Why do you think that you will?"

"Or look at it from a different point of view. Do you know someone who lost his job at the age of thirty-eight and never got a job till retirement?"

John thought for a while and answered "No."

I went on asking, "Do you think that you will be the first man not to find a job until retirement? Please think objectively."

John sighed heavily and said, "I don't suppose I will be the first."

I kept on probing. "Do you know that most people who lose their jobs, find a new job with better salary, better benefits, a better work environment or better potential for promotion, or all of the above? Most of them would never dream of going back to their old jobs. It all depends on how you look at being out of a job. You can look at it as a disaster or as a great opportunity. It will be what you want it to be."

"You cling to your job because you are used to it. Staying in your present position makes you feels secure. You think that going outside to look for another job is scary, that there is nothing better there. This reminds me of the old Yiddish proverb, 'The worm that lives in the horseradish thinks there is nothing sweeter in the world.' In a way, we all live in a 'horseradish' and do not want to leave it. That is probably the most important reason why so many people, who are not happy with their jobs, do not leave them until someone lays them off and forces them to look for a new job outside. As soon as you will get out of your 'horseradish' and look around, you will find many sweeter things and would never even consider going back to your old job." However, John was inconsolable. No matter what I said, he remained miserable. From a rational point of view he probably understood that I was right, but emotionally he could not accept it.

He told me that he thought that he finally had a secure job, where he would accumulate enough money in the pension plan and eventually retire. Now though, everything had changed.

"I do not like changes; they bring new headaches." said John.

I told him that change is an integral part of life and that he should take advantage of it. He should embrace change with enthusiasm rather than resent it. "You are a young man. There will be more changes in your life. Learn how to live with change and make it work for you." I said.

I finally understood that the shock was too great, and that now was not the time to bring him to his senses. Perhaps after two or three days he would look at it from a more rational point of view. At the end of our conversation, I asked him to call me in six months and tell me how things were going.

For the next day or two, John was so sure he was right, that he was not satisfied with explaining his predicament just to me. He went to anybody who was willing to listen and told him his story, stressing that he wanted to know why the company laid him off. In truth, he had few attentive listeners. Employees and managers listened to him politely but tried to distance themselves from him as if he were a pariah. It seemed as if they were afraid that being close to him would put them in danger of losing their jobs. Judging by their behavior you would think that losing a job was a contagious disease.

I later learned that John sued the company and lost. He had to pay an undisclosed amount of dollars to the company for legal expenses. It reminded me of the man who cut off his nose to spite his face.

On the sunny side, John called me a few months later to tell me that he had thought a great deal, about our conversation, and started viewing his problem as an opportunity. After exhaustive searches, he accepted an offer to become a president of a small company, which was looking for someone with production management experience. While the company was small, he was getting a salary forty percent higher than his old one, plus a share of the profits, which in a good year could double his pay. What made him most proud though was the new Cadillac that the company has leased for him, so he would make a good impression when visiting customers. At the end of our conversation, he said to me, "I want you to know Henry, you were the only person who told me the truth."

A few months later, Jack, our corporate executive vice president based in Detroit, visited our division, and was disappointed that monthly sales were lower than our forecasts. I had explained to him many times in the past, that while the forecast for the year was accurate, the monthly forecast was often inaccurate because a big order from an important customer that was expected this month could arrive a few days late making this month look bad and the next month look good. He kept on nagging me about monthly sales time and again, until finally I told him, that we needed his help for the monthly forecast, because we did not know how to do it ourselves.

Jack did not respond, but I could tell from his expression that he was upset. The reason was simple: He did not know how to make accurate monthly forecasts either. No one knows. Looking at his face, I sensed immediately that I had made a mistake, but I was so upset that I did nothing to correct it.

One month later, our divisional president called me to his office and told me that they decided to "eliminate" my position. In other words, he laid me off. He wanted to explain to me why, but I said that I am not interested in the reasons, and that as the president he has the right to lay me off just because he does not want me on his team.

He tried to persuade me that I should listen to the reasons but I refused. I remembered what happened to John who wanted to know why, and I figured that if I asked for reasons, they would find some. After all, no one is perfect, and if they would try to persuade me that their reasons were valid, they would in the process convince themselves that I am not a good manager. I could not see how this would make things better for me.

It is my belief that the president actually liked me. I suspected that Jack, the corporate executive vice president had something to do with me being laid-off. I was given two weeks to tie-up the loose ends and clear out my belongings.

On the first day, I was shocked and scared. What was I going to do? After all, I had a wife and three children to support. True, I had always wanted to be a consultant, but I had hoped to do it gradually, first part-time, while I still had a steady income and then full-time after I had enough clients. Soon afterwards, though, I said to myself that this was a test of my strength. I decided that I would not let this crisis break me. I made it a challenge to myself to overcome this difficulty and come out of this crisis stronger and better than before. If I could give good advice to John, why not apply it to myself? Did I not always tell people, "If life gives you lemons make lemonade?" Was it just talk on my part or could I live by it?

I convinced myself that this was a great opportunity for me to try something new, and that I should not waste it. I said to myself that self-pity would get me nowhere. Instead of bemoaning my misery, I should sit down and develop a course of action. A day later, I did just that. I ordered business cards and letterheads, and developed a list of potential clients to call. I began developing a strategy for acquiring new clients.

At work, I acted normally. I was cheerful and courteous to everyone as if nothing had happened. I smiled and behaved like a happy man and tried to help others solve work-related problems. I even submitted a report to the president on a project that I had started six weeks earlier, showing him how we could save over ninety two thousand dollars. I realized that leaving on good terms was important to me. My grandmother used to say that you could catch more flies with honey than with vinegar. I still believe it.

I was amazed how many friends I had among the employees. Many of them came to me expressing their sorrow at my departure and asked how they could help me. I thanked them profusely and promised to take them up on their offer as soon as the opportunity arose.

After a week, the president called me to his office. He asked me what I was planning to do.

"I will start a consulting business helping companies grow, improve systems and reduce costs using my interactive management method, just as I did for you. Do you remember my first project? You told me that you needed more money for investment in machinery but your bank refused to increase your credit line. My answer to you was, "Why go to the bank? Pick up money from your floor!" I still remember your puzzled look. We then redesigned the inventory control system, reduced inventory levels and cut labor cost on the most important products through a better layout and improved methods. In a few months, you had all the cash you needed. You even started taking 2% discounts for invoices paid in ten days whenever possible, something you had not done for years! There may be many other companies in a similar position, and I want to help them."

The president frowned, thought for a moment and then asked me, "Would you take us on as a client?"

I could not believe my ears. Was this possible? Could I be so lucky as to walk out of here with my first client?

"Of course" I answered. "That is what I am in business for."

That is how I started my consulting company. I started out working only one day a week, but after two weeks I already had two days of work a week and after a month, three days a week.

After only one month, I was making more working three days a week as a consultant, than I had earned in my position as a vice president working five days a week.

I stayed with this client for seven years as a consultant, until the company was sold and the president lost his job. A few years later, the president opened his own company and took me on as a consultant for a number of projects. I am still working there.

I am reminded of the words of Franklin D. Roosevelt, that the only thing we have to fear is fear itself. If you know someone who was laid-off, be sure to tell him this story.

I still feel bad that I did not send the president twelve roses and a thank you note when he laid me off. He certainly deserved it. He earned it.

Chapter 2

The Pairing of Options Principle

> I am an old man and have known a great many troubles, but most of them never happened.
> — *Mark Twain*

We do things the way we do, because we view things in our own, special way. Were we to view the issues from another perspective, they would look different to us and we would act upon them differently. The way we perceive our business, our customers and our products often makes the difference between success and failure.

For example, our fears and worries often prevent us from acting. Yet, by some estimates, 95% of the things we worry about never happen, and another 4% will happen no matter what we do. Thus, we could eliminate 99% of our worries. Viewed from this perspective, our fears are less likely to influence our decisions and actions.

Some managers are afraid to make decisions. It is important to remember that not making a decision, because we are afraid of consequences, is also a decision that has consequences. These consequences are sometimes worse than the ones we wanted to prevent.

Thinking this way can help us sort out our options in a sagging economy. We must increase productivity and profits to survive. Yet, many companies try accomplishing this in an ineffective way. They often view the issues and problems from the same perspective year after year, not realizing that the world around them changes all the time.

They try to improve systems that were appropriate ten years ago, and find it difficult to understand that making these outdated systems more efficient is not enough to compete in today's marketplace.

I am reminded of the old horse and carriage driver who, reacting to the emergence of the new motorized and elegantly appointed taxicabs, decided to buy a stronger horse and upholster the carriage in order to attract more customers. He tried to improve the outdated system, because that was the system he felt comfortable with, and which he knew thoroughly. It is easy for us to understand that the old driver looked at the issue from the wrong perspective and therefore, chose an inappropriate course of action. This is because the problems of others are often easier to spot than our own.

When it comes to issues we face in daily business situations, we tend to behave in the same manner as the old driver, unless we have someone to help us see the issues from new perspectives.

Although we often think there are only a few alternatives, a little thought and reflection will uncover many perspectives from which to view an issue. Each perspective will produce new alternatives.

Consider a simple experiment. Think of a business problem, and find ten managers who are competent enough to solve it. Lock each one in a room by himself. Ask each of them to solve the problem, and give you his solution by the end of the day.

How many different solutions would you get? If you guessed ten you are probably right. Two or three of the solutions would probably be good, two would probably be so bad that they could drive you out of business; another four to six would be mediocre.

The question that begs an answer is why might ten competent managers arrive at ten different solutions to the same problem.

One reason could be that the ten managers had ten different perspectives from which they looked at the problem and its possible solution. Their perspectives were different because they had different experiences, different educations and different backgrounds. This diversity is very beneficial. It increases the chances that you will find a much better solution than if you had only one or two solutions to choose from. This diversity is the engine of progress in all fields of human endeavor. Just imagine what the world would be like if we all thought alike. It is this diversity that caused the managers to arrive at ten different solutions.

Whatever solution you choose will have a great impact on your success. Since some of the solutions are more conducive to the achievement of your stated objectives than others, it is imperative that you choose the solution, which is most appropriate to your problem. However, without reviewing a substantial number of options the probability that your course of action would be close to the optimum is quite low. If we took not ten but a hundred managers, we would probably get close to a hundred solutions. I often wondered: If I were one of the hundred, what would be the probability that the most appropriate solution would be mine?

The probability would certainly be low. Yet, most of the time, we simply assume that our solution is the best and we act accordingly. This may be the result of constant pressure and lack of time to think through the various perspectives and analyze them properly. Alternatively, perhaps our ego gets in our way and we are reluctant to admit that our perspectives are not the best. Either way, our chosen course of action is often close to the lower end of the spectrum and the result is that we do so many things backwards.

If you agree with what we have said until now, then every time you make an important decision you should ask yourself: How am I viewing this problem? Are there other perspectives to view it from? How many other perspectives can I think of? There are no easy answers to these questions. It is not easy to think of perspectives that do not come to us naturally, because each of us is a prisoner surrounded by the walls of our perceptions and prejudices created by our experiences, education and background.

It would be easier to get many options if we could get input from other people whom we respect and trust, providing that we could subdue our ego, and admit that other options could be better than our own. This is not easy either.

Assuming you could overcome the above difficulties and now have ten options to choose from. How do you decide which option is best for you? I have designed the following method for my clients, which I call the pairing of options principle. In many cases, it will not only help you choose correctly, but can even help you develop a better option than the ten options you started from.

As we have said before, once you have to consider many additional perspectives and the resulting courses of action, you will tend to feel confused. Sorting through many options can be overwhelming. However, there is a secret to analyzing multiple options. First, find as many options as feasible and then pair the various options. Now you can work on one pair at a time, analyze the advantages and disadvantages of each option in the pair, and perhaps, in the process, develop a third option, which has more advantages and less drawbacks than the original two.

To make things more concrete, let us assume we have only four options and call them A, B, C and D. Let one pair be A and B, and the other pair C and D.

Take a sheet of paper and divide it into four wide columns, two for A and two for B. In the first column, write the good features of A, and in the second column write the bad features. Do the same thing for option B. Can you develop an option E that has most of the good features of A and of B and the least of the bad features of the two options? Often this can be done using a logical process.

If we start with four options or courses of action, and work on them in pairs, we will wind up with two improved courses of action. Option E will be generated as the synthesis of A and B, as explained above, and option F as the synthesis of C and D. Repeating the process with the improved pair, E and F, and generating option G, can yield an even better result, much as cross-breeding is used to breed a better horse or cow. It should be noted that G is not necessarily the best option, however, it certainly is not the worst one because there are at least six worse options. A case study based on the pairing of options is described in the chapter entitled "The Bull's Eye Principle".

Try this approach and you may be surprised at how well it works. Productivity and profits often can be improved in a matter of weeks with minimum investment. This Pairing of Options approach recently helped a window company increase productivity by 22%, capacity by 40% and profits by 78% in less than ten weeks. These results were achieved by helping managers, supervisors and employees view two important issues from new perspectives, finding new options, applying the pairing of options principle to develop the most desirable option, and by concentrating their attention and resources on the important issues with the single-mindedness of purpose necessary for obtaining significant results in a relatively short period of time.

One of the issues was the supervisors' eagerness to increase output and productivity. They decided to increase the output of saw operators and punch-press operators, hoping that this would push welders, sash assemblers and final assemblers to produce faster.

The supervisors explained their point of view convincingly: "If you feed them more they will eat more." To reinforce their argument they added, "If they do not receive more parts, they certainly cannot produce more." Viewed from this perspective, their action made good sense. However, looking at the actual results, they saw that the new avalanche of parts clogged the assembly lines creating bottlenecks and confusion. This resulted in a waste of time searching for the right parts for each order, and actually reduced the output, rather than increase it as they had hoped. This reminds me of William H. Swanson's rule, "Constantly review developments to make sure that the actual benefits are what they were supposed to be." Once they viewed their problems and goals from a new perspective, they developed a better course of action, and achieved results closer to their stated objectives.

What we can learn from this example is that when a decision-maker takes a narrow-minded look at new alternatives for coping with the changing needs of his organization, when because of time pressures, he implements the first solution that comes to mind, rather than comparing several options and choosing the most appropriate one, his action may cause a reaction that is harmful to business as we saw in the example above.

Chapter 3

The Bull's Eye Principle

The greatest pleasure in life is doing what people say you cannot do.

— *Walter Bagehot*

The following story has a great lesson for anyone connected with management. It helped me develop my interactive consulting method, described in the second part of this chapter.

Tom and Jack had not seen each other for fifteen years. There was a lot that they had to say to one another to make up for lost time. Jack had become very wealthy and wanted to impress Tom with his new estate, so he invited him to come see it. The estate was only ten minutes away, so they decided to walk. As they came closer, Tom saw a long brick wall surrounding the estate. On the wall, he noticed hundreds of targets, with a bullet right in the center of each bull's-eye.

"Who managed to get the bullets in to the center every time?" asked Tom.

"I did." replied Jack modestly.

"Then you must be an excellent marksman," said Tom. "How did you do it?"

"Simple" said Jack "First I shot the bullet, and then I drew the target".

At first glance, this seems to be completely backwards. That is not what shooting is all about. In fact, what Jack did is to turn the problem upside down. A closer analysis will show however, that the story is not as crazy as it seems.

Let's first rephrase the problem and ask, "What is the easiest way to get a bullet into the center of a target"? Surely, the answer is, "You shoot first and then draw the target around the bullet." Now our story sounds more reasonable. It suggests a good solution to the problem at hand. In fact, the best solutions to method improvements are often found when we turn problems upside down, sideways or backwards, perhaps because we do so many things backwards to begin with.

You may remember from your history studies the tale of the Gordian knot, which was tied by King Gordius of Phrygia. An oracle revealed that whoever untied the knot and separated the two ropes would be the future master of Asia. Many warriors tried to separate the ropes, but could not untie the knot. Alexander the Great also tried his luck, but even he could not untie the knot. However, Alexander the Great was not a man to accept failure easily, so he turned things upside down and did them in a non-conventional way: he cut the knot with his sword and separated the two ropes. The oracle immediately predicted that he would be the master of Asia.

Trying to do things in an unconventional way often yields excellent results. You may remember the Biblical story of how King Solomon decided who was the rightful mother of a child claimed by each of two women as her own. When all investigations and persuasions failed, the King decided to bring a sword to cut the child in two and divide it between the women. One woman said, "Cut it, neither of us will have it alive." The other woman cried "No! Give her the child, but do not harm it." Immediately the King announced, "The latter one is the rightful mother."

Two examples of unconventional approaches come to mind from my own experience. One case has to do with the old method of producing windows before computers were used in manufacture.

I was working for a company that produced windows for homeowners. When a homeowner ordered windows for his house, the salesman measured the windows after closing the sale. He started from one end of the house and measured each window as he walked around the house. Some windows were large and some were small. To save time and work, the salesman wrote the window sizes on an order form that had six copies. The six copies were for: (a) production scheduling (b) the saw operator (c) production of the insulated glass (d) production of windows on the assembly line (e) invoicing and (f) company records.

The glass came to the line, leaning on L shaped pallets, in descending size order with the largest pane leaning on the L pallet in the back and the smallest in the front, to prevent glass breakage. The vinyl to produce the sash arrived at the assembly line precut, sticking out of wooden boxes arranged in the order written on the salesman's measuring sheet.

The assemblers were instructed to assemble the windows in the order they appeared on the production sheet, and to make a check mark on the sheet after each window was completed. When every window on the sheet had a check mark, the order was complete.

The system worked like this for many years, but had one drawback. The glass, which was arranged by size, often cracked because the assemblers had to pull the pane of glass from somewhere in the middle of the pallet, based on the order written on the production sheet.

Then someone noticed that the glass could only be accessed sequentially, like records of a sequential access file. Namely, you could not get to the pane in the middle of the pallet without handling all the smaller panes stored in front of it. It would always be easier and safer to take the pane of glass stored in the front of the pallet than any other pane. This would prevent the glass from breaking. The precut vinyl to produce the sash could be accessed randomly like records of a random access file. Namely, you could pull any piece of vinyl without disturbing the other pieces. It, therefore, made sense to turn the system upside down and produce the windows not in the order of the salesman's measuring sheet, but rather by increasing glass size. This way the assembler would always take the glass from the front of the pallet. In other words, instead of pulling the pane of glass that matched the order as written by the salesman, the assemblers would simply take the smallest pane of glass stored in front of the pallet and then pull the corresponding sash members.

This saved a lot of glass breakage and was much easier and faster. The assemblers had to be retrained to check off the windows not in the order of production sheet but rather in the order of glass. At the end, they also had to verify that all the windows on the sheet were checked off.

The following case study is even a better example of the bull's-eye principle. It saved about 80% of labor cost. It deals with fruit packing at a fruit packinghouse.

The packinghouse had to meet specifications of the retail stores. When the fruit was delivered, the merchants required that it be neatly arranged in the crate. When the merchant displayed the newly opened crate, the fruit had to be arranged in straight rows. Once the crate was opened, and the customers began taking the fruit out, the arrangement was not important since the first customer would disturb the order anyway, trying to get to the fruit at the bottom, which he thought might be nicer. It was the first impression that counted.

Faced with these demands, the workers in the packinghouse were required to diligently arrange the fruit in the crate neatly layer by layer, sometimes eight or nine layers deep, depending on the size of the fruit. When the crate was full, it moved on a conveyor to be closed, by nailing the upper lid on top of the crate.

This was a labor-intensive and time-consuming operation because every fruit in the crate was handled manually. Then someone thought of a crazy idea. His reasoning was simple. If all we need is to present the upper layer neatly when the box is opened, why bother to arrange the whole box neatly?

To accomplish this the operation was turned literally upside down. The crates came to the line with nailed tops but without bottoms. Before filling it with fruit, the top of the crate was marked "This side up". Next, the crate was turned upside down and filled with fruit with the top of the crate resting on the table and the open bottom facing up. The first layer of fruit was arranged neatly because it rested on the side of the crate that was marked "This side up". After neatly arranging the first layer, the fruit was thrown into the crate haphazardly or even directly from a sack. Care was taken to pack the fruit tightly so that the layer resting on the cover would not move. Then the bottom of the crate was nailed on and the crate was again turned upside down with the top facing up ready for shipment.

Another example of turning problems upside down is the interactive consulting method I developed. I used to work for a conventional consulting company. We would go to a client's plant, analyze the operation, the systems and the procedures. We would take them apart and put them together the best way we could think of. Then we would put all our findings into a thick report of about 200 pages. The report was leather-bound with golden lettering on the cover. The report was always impressive. It was a testimony to the many hours that we spent in the client's company and justification of our high fees. It was also a sign that we had completed the assignment and had earned our fee.

We would give enough copies to the president, for himself and for management. We found that the president and some top managers would usually read the report. The consulting company would send me a month later for a follow up visit, to answer questions, if any, and to see if they needed help with any other projects.

What I usually found was that most managers did not read the report in depth. Those who did often made sure that the recommendations contained in the report would not be implemented. In the end, the report would collect dust on a shelf. I began to ask myself, "What are we doing wrong?"

Ironically, the consulting company did well. However, I was interested in tangible results not just in collection of fees. Unfortunately, I found out the hard way, that after submitting the report, I had no control over what companies did with it.

After some years in the consulting business, I became so frustrated that I decided to quit and go into operations. Two years later, I was promoted to the position of vice-president in a Fortune 500 division. We were growing enormously, and I could not do everything myself, so I hired consultants to help me. These were reputable people known for their sharp minds.

They analyzed the operations, systems and procedures, put them together in the best way they knew how, summarizing everything in a thick report, leather bound with golden lettering. The engineer who wrote the report proudly signed his name on it, and gave me ten copies of the report to distribute to my managers.

When I gave the report to the managers, the same thing happened as when I was a consultant. Now though, circumstances were reversed. The resistance to the report was very strong. The managers did not attack the consultants directly, because they came to us highly recommended. Instead, they would say that the consultants were smart people but could not learn the small details of the operation in the limited time they were here. Their recommendations might be good for other places, but here they would not work.

I always wondered why managers had such a strong resistance to the consultants' recommendations. What were the consultants doing wrong?

One day a manager of mine quit. I was a little surprised and I invited him for an exit interview over a cup of coffee. I wanted to learn from him whether perhaps I did something wrong that prompted him to quit. I do not like to make the same mistake twice if I can help it.

As we talked, I tried to learn from him why the managers and supervisors were so opposed to the consultants' recommendations. He did not say it in so many words, but I understood from him that the consultant and the old-timer manager viewed the consulting report from different perspectives. To the consultant the report was a blueprint for implementation. It often included an implementation schedule: what to do on Monday what to do on Tuesday and so on. Ideally, if someone followed the recommendations, he could not fail.

To the old-timer the report was something quite different. Far from being a blueprint for implementation, the report was simply a monument to the wisdom of the consultant. "Did you see those beautiful charts? Did you understand the complex multicolor graphs and mathematical equations? He must be a smart fellow. He spent only six months here and found all the solutions. I have been here twenty years, and I could not even find the problems. What will the president think of me? If the consultant's solutions should work, heaven forbid, the president will think that I must be a moron. Will he lay me off? Will he demote me? Maybe he will freeze me in my present position and present salary for life? I must do something in a hurry before it is too late."

The truth is that an intelligent president does not expect his staff to design a better system using quantifying methods and other modern engineering techniques. He would be pleased if his people were able to work with the consultant and could learn the new methods to run their departments more effectively. However, the old-timer does not know that, and when it comes to his job security he cannot take any chances. The self-preservation instinct instantly kicks in. This is the strongest instinct we have and it overrides all other considerations. In any event, the old-timer does not stand to gain anything from the consultant's work, so why take unnecessary risks?

I could also see that the supervisors and managers had an unwritten covenant to help each other. The reasoning was simple but powerful, "If the consultant should succeed in one department, they would soon ask him to work in another department, and eventually in my department. The sooner the consultant is out the door, the better for everybody."

Ironically though, I found that the better the recommendations, the stronger the resistance of managers and supervisors. If the recommendations were bad and would fail miserably, everyone would be glad to implement them. They would then be able to say to the president: "We told you so. There was no need for an outside consultant. After many years of experience, we know the business better than any outsider."

That cup of coffee I had with the manager taught me a great deal. I understood for the first time why consultants, even the best ones, fail in implementation. There seems to be a competition between the consultant and the old-timer. They both want the credit for any improvements. The consultant has the report to show off his good ideas. This makes the old-timer feel inadequate. The old-timer thinks that if the consultant's recommendations are good and he wins, than he, the old-timer looks inadequate and, therefore loses. In this battle between the consultant and managers, it is easy to predict who will win. The consultant would like to succeed, but to him it is not a matter of life or death. He collects his fee when he submits his report. To him the success of implementation is only a secondary matter. He can always blame poor management for lack of implementation. The old-timer looks at things differently. To him winning is a matter of survival, or so he thinks. He must win in order to maintain his job, his livelihood. If he should lose, he may be laid-off. In that case, he would be devastated.

His wife and children may lose the respect for him as a breadwinner. His whole world would crumble. His self-preservation instinct is mobilized to ensure he wins. In any situation like this, the instinct of self-preservation will prevail.

The other problem is that the recommendations of consultants do not always work out well. This is to be expected. Even best laid plans can fail in implementation, especially if there are many people who want them to fail. However, the truth is that the old-timer often knows what needs to be done better than the consultant does. Many consultants are afraid to admit it, fearing that the client will think that he does not need them. Even worse, the consultant sometimes takes ideas from an old-timer and presents the ideas as his own. Nothing infuriates an old-timer more than stealing credit from him.

I said to myself, there must be a better way. The consultants are doing it all backwards. The process must be turned upside down to alleviate the following problems:

- The old-timer's fear of losing his job because he thinks that he is competing with the consultant and one of them must lose

- The consultant's inadequate knowledge of the details of a particular operation

- The old timer's resistance to change

I started to experiment with different methods. I also kept in mind that many improvements were not being implemented because they were "not invented here." I finally designed the interactive consulting method to fulfill the following requirements:

- People who will have to live with the improvements must be the ones who invent them. The interactive consultant may help them invent the improvements, but they must know and understand all the details involved. This will eliminate the fear of the unknown, which causes the resistance to change.

- The credit for the improvements must go to the people who invent them and help implement them. Their bosses and peers should recognize their contribution. Thus the employees, proud of their achievements, will embrace the changes with enthusiasm rather than with resentment.

- Whenever feasible, the employees who invent or help implement the improvements should get some remuneration like a promotion, an increase in wages, a bonus or the like. This will answer their natural question of "What's in it for me?" and help them embrace the changes with enthusiasm.

- The consultant must treat all employees, supervisors and managers with respect. He must give them the feeling that they know more about their department than he does, and that he is willing to learn from them. Thus they will not be afraid that the consultant will outshine them.

- The employees that have to live with the improvements must feel that the project is their own. If the project succeeds, it is their success. If the project fails it is their failure. The consultant is here only to help them succeed.
- Whenever possible, reports should be written **after** the improvements are implemented not before.

The last point requires some explanation. Many consultants' problems stem from the fact that their recommendations do not work. This could be the result of their lack of knowledge of the operation, bad relations with managers and employees who want the consultant to fail, or other reasons. The only way to make sure that the report includes only what works is to reverse the order. First implement the improvements and then include only the items that work in the report. You might say that this is like first shooting and then drawing the target around the bullet – you can never miss. Well, you are right, it is an application of the bull's eye principle. If you think that this not fair, consider the following question: What is the point of writing a report with recommendations that might not work?

When the report is written **after** the improvements are working, it is a completely different type of report. It is not a blueprint for implementation as the conventional consultant's report, but rather a summary of what was implemented and a means of giving credit where it is due, because the names of the participating employees appear on the cover of the report.

This may seem like putting the carriage in front of the horse, but it works like a charm. It has a few important advantages. First, no one can claim that the recommendations in the report will not work. They are already working, sometimes for two or three months. Secondly, there is no one left to resist the report because the managers and employees who would usually resist it are among the authors who recommended the improvements.

In the beginning, the managers may resist the interactive consultant's approach. They may suspect that he is just another consultant, who tries to gain their trust and later talk them into something that is bad for them. However, with a little skill their resistance fades away, as evident from the following case.

The company had about 250 employees. The president of the company introduced me to a group of twenty managers and supervisors. I asked each participant his name and how long he had been working for the company. Some had been there for twenty years, many had been there over ten years; only two had been with the company for less than a year.

"I've been here less than ten minutes," I said to them. "If anyone knows what to do here, it cannot be me it has to be you."

There was quiet in the room. Every one was surprised. Soon however, the instinct of survival got the better of them. They still remembered how hard they had struggled to get the previous consultant out two years ago.

Jack said, "You mean to say that you do not know what to do here; you do not know the answers?"

"You heard me correctly. I do not know the answers. How could I? I have been here only ten minutes. If I am lucky, I will stay here for a few months. How do you expect me to know what you have learned in ten or twenty years?"

Phillip chimed in, "But if you do not know what to do here, if you do not know the answers, how are you going to help us?"

"I do not know the answers, but I do know the questions. If I will ask you the right questions, you will come up with the right answers."

"But if we already know the answers why do we need you to ask the questions. Why do we need you at all?"

I was taken aback by this logic. It took me a second or two to regain my composure.

I said to Phillip, "When was it the last time that you saw a man running down the street screaming 'I have a wonderful answer. Who has a question?' It never happens, because people do not give answers unless someone first asks a question. You will see how it all works in a week or two."

"You mean to say that you will ask the questions, we will give the answers and then you will take our ideas and put them into your report as your own, as the other consultant did two years ago?"

"No," I said. "I do not write reports, I do not make recommendations and I do not tell people what to do. The projects will be yours. If there will be reports, they will be yours. Your name will be on the cover. You will get all the credit. If you succeed, you will all shine like stars. If you fail, the yolk will be on your faces. Do not worry though; I will help you succeed. I want you all to shine like stars. As the company grows there will be promotions, there will be pay increases, and I want you to get them."

Some were convinced but most of them were skeptical. They thought that this was another ploy to gain their confidence. Fortunately, one of the supervisors was willing to try, so I started with him. His name was Peter. He suggested that we start with Tom, whose job was to assemble locks.

I asked Tom how long he had worked on this particular operation. He told me that he had been doing it for over five years. I remarked that if he had been doing it for five years, then whatever he was doing had to be good. I asked him to show me what he was doing.

The operation was simple. He took part A and B and assembled them into a subassembly C. Then he created subassembly F from parts D and E. Subassemblies C and F were assembled into the finished product, packed in a box and put on a pallet across the aisle. Actually, the operation was more complex, but we will omit some details for the sake of simplicity. I asked Tom why he did it in this particular way. He answered that the people in the company always did it this way. Besides, this was how they trained him when he first started this job.

I asked Tom if he ever thought of another method of assembling the lock. He said that he never had. I said to him, "You know this operation better than anyone in this company, even better than the president. If anybody can improve this operation, it can only be you. You are a smart man. Here is what you can do: think of three other ways to do this operation. They do not have to be necessarily better than the present way, just different. To succeed you must concentrate on this problem. Who knows you may even think of something better.

This is not important though. Just think of something different. I will be here next week and we will see what we can do."

When I came next week Tom called me proudly to his workbench and explained to me the three different methods he thought of. One was even slightly better than the present method. Now we had four ways to perform the operation, including the present one.

We were ready to roll. I explained to Tom and to Peter his supervisor, the pairing of options method. "Let us call the four methods we have **A**, **B**, **C**, and **D**. We will work on one pair at a time. Take **A** and **B**. Think what are the good and bad features of **A**. Then think what are the good and bad features of **B**. Take a sheet of paper and draw four columns. A good and bad column for method **A** and a good and bad column for method **B**. List the good and bad features of **A** and **B** on the sheet. I will come here next week and review the sheet with you. You have done an excellent job till now, so I am sure that you will do well in listing the features."

When I came next week I found that Tom and Peter listed the good and bad features of **A** and **B**. By asking a few questions, I helped them discover additional features and better define the features they had listed. I asked Tom to create a method **E** for next week, by combining as many good features as possible of **A** and **B**, and eliminating as many bad features as possible.

Sure enough, next week Tom presented me with method **E**. By definition, method **E** was better than **A** and **B**. I said to Tom "You did such a great job with method **A** and **B** that you will have no difficulty doing the same for **C** and **D**. In three weeks, we had method **F** that by definition was better than **C** and **D**. Finally; I helped Tom do the same with the improved pair **E** and **F**, which yielded option **G**, which we called the "Good option." I could see that Tom and Peter were quite pleased.

Please keep in mind that option **G** was not necessarily the best option available. There may have been better options that we did not think of. At the very least though, we knew that **G** was not the worst option. We knew that, by definition, there were at least six options worse than **G**. This is something that we could not have said about the previous method. It could have been from the bottom of the barrel.

We decided to implement method **G** and see how it worked. To allay Tom's fear of failure we agreed that if the method did not work we would not tell anyone about it. We would simply think of something else that did work, and only then would we let everyone know. This made it a no risk proposition.

In the beginning the new method did not work well. There were bugs to iron out and changes to make in the way the parts were delivered and placed on the bench. We also had to redesign the bench. Even though the new method did not work well, Tom did not give up. He wanted to show that his new method was better than the old one. After four weeks, the new method was completely debugged and fully operational.

The savings were impressive. There were 34% savings in labor and a 25% improvement in quality. Tom also claimed that he was less tired in the evening. I asked Tom and Peter whether the president and vice president knew what they had accomplished. They said that they probably did not. I stressed that it was important that they knew what a good job Peter and Tom did in improving the operation. After all, there would be wage increases and promotions in the future.

"What shall I do?" asked Tom. "I cannot barge to the president's office and toot my horn."

"This will not be necessary," I answered. "Write a brief report on what you have done, and I will make sure that everyone gets a copy."

First Tom said that he had no time to write reports. Then he admitted that he was not sure he knew how to write one.

"No problem," I said. "I have the time, and I know how to write reports. Let me write a draft for you. Cross out what you do not like and add what I have missed. Remember it is your report." Tom agreed. I have never encountered anyone who refused such a generous risk-free offer with everything to gain and nothing to lose.

A week later, I handed Tom the draft with his name and Peter's name as authors on the cover. They made minor corrections and added that it was not fair for them to take all the credit. After all, I had helped them. They suggested that I put my name on the cover too. I put my name under theirs.

I made twenty copies of the report and gave a copy to every executive and manager in the company. I also went to the president and vice president and suggested that they visit Tom's new operation and give him the proverbial pat on the back for a job well done, something that Tom and Peter earned. They did so. I asked the president when Tom was due for a yearly review. He called personnel and said that Tom was due for a review in five months.

I suggested to the president that in view of Tom's accomplishments, he should get a wage increase now and the next review would be a year from now. The same should be done for Peter. The president agreed.

I made sure that the company newspaper reporter interviewed Tom and Peter for an article. I supplied the newspaper with color pictures of Tom performing the various operations, with Peter looking on. Tom and Peter became celebrities overnight and everyone knew who they were and what they had accomplished.

A week later, the president called me to his office and said "I almost fell off my chair yesterday because of you".

I asked, "Why? What did I do wrong?"

"Nothing", said the president. "Charlie, the manager of inventory control department evidently saw what happened to Tom and Peter and asked me to send you to help him as well. I could not believe my ears. I have had consultants here before. The managers and supervisors could not wait for them to leave. For a manager to ask the president to send him a consultant is simply unbelievable. I never heard of such a thing."

I explained to the president that this often happens in my interactive consulting method. This method helps employees develop better solutions, gives them credit for their input, and helps them be rewarded for their contribution. From the employee's point of view this a risk-free proposition. He can only win.

I worked with Charlie on inventory control and I helped him implement my "Inventory Cardiogram" method, which was featured in Inc., Success, and many other magazines. Charlie improved his management skills considerably and was ready for his next promotion. He became a vice president of the company. Materials management was only one of his departments. He kept me busy with various projects in the company for many years.

You can use the interactive consulting method even if you are not a consultant. As a manager, you can use it to implement changes more easily. Part of managing is helping your people think of new ideas. You will be surprised how interactive consulting can make your job easier.

Even if you are not a consultant or manager you can use the interactive consulting approach. If you are a salesman you can use it with your customers. Help them solve their problems. Do not tell them what to do, ask them. Let them give the answer. You can also use this method when dealing with your spouse or children. Help them think of better ways of doing things, give credit where due and be generous with praise and thanks for their ideas, just as you should do with your employees.

Employees are starved for praise and credit. If they do something right they seldom hear a word of praise. It is taken for granted. After all this is what they are paid for. However if they do something wrong they soon hear about it; everybody criticizes them. Sometimes they are demoted or even laid-off. The result is that employees hear more bad things about their performance than good things. That is exactly where interactive consulting can help you improve the situation and make everyone feel good about himself. You may need a little practice to become good at it, but it is worth the effort.

You can start by giving credit to everyone who deserves it and thank everyone who does a good job for you. This happens about ten times a day. You may think that everyone should do a good job, because that is what he is paid to do. This is not true. Look at it from a different perspective. It is true that a man works for you to make money. However, it is also true that he could make the same money working for somebody else. You simply owe him thanks for choosing to work for you. If you do not give him enough credit and a good feeling about himself he will sooner or later look for a job somewhere else.

After a little practice, you will find many applications for interactive consulting in whatever you do. It will make you feel better and make your life easier. It will also make everyone around you feel better about you and about themselves.

I have been using my interactive consulting method for twenty-five years for businesses of all sizes, from small businesses to Fortune 500 companies. I have used interactive consulting in a wide variety of environments, including office operations, customer service, marketing and sales promotion, strategy planning and manufacturing. Interactive consulting has proven effective in a variety of businesses and industries, at all levels of management from presidents of companies down to supervisors, and I've never had a project that was not successful. I asked myself how is this possible? Nothing is perfect. Is it just sheer luck that I was successful for twenty-five years? Will I fail next time? Then it dawned on me that if you work with my interactive method and you know what you are doing it is nearly impossible to fail. In order for me to fail all managers and supervisors who work on projects with me would have to fail also. They would never let this happen; their instinct of survival would not let them. Ironically, the same instinct that causes the conventional consultant to fail, assures my success.

You can also look at it from a different perspective. Under the prevalent consulting approach, the old timer believes that if the consultant's recommendations are good and the project succeeds the consultant will look like a smart fellow and be a winner but he, the old timer, who could not find the solutions or even the problems, will look incompetent and, therefore, be a loser. On the other hand, if the consultant's recommendations are shown not to be good and the project fails, the old timer, who says that consultants are waste of money, perceives himself as a winner and the consultant as a loser. It is a "win-lose" situation, in which one party must lose for the other to win. Hence, the old timer has every incentive to make sure that the project fails and he "wins."

Under the interactive consulting system, if the project is successful the old timer is a hero and both he and the consultant are winners. It is a "win-win" situation. If the project fails, they both lose. Therefore, the old timer has every incentive to make sure that the project succeeds. Thus, my interactive method is probably as foolproof as can be.

The bull's eye principal is very powerful. I used it many times to turn problems upside down with excellent results. Perhaps the reason the bull's eye principle is so successful is that, as we noted before, we do so many things backwards to begin with.

Chapter 4

Keep It Simple

> I have always wished for my computer to be as easy to use as my telephone; my wish has come true because I can no longer figure out how to use my telephone.
> — *Bjarne Stroustrup*

When helping companies cope with the ever-expanding selection of management information systems (MIS) available, I am often reminded of the story of George the "genius".

Omega was a small company producing high quality doors. The company was making good money, but management was embarrassed that they did not have a "real" computer system on premises. Actually, they did have a computer that they had acquired a few years before, but it was an old system that was not really used much, certainly nothing to brag about in the modern day and age. The president thought that they ought to be more efficient and more automated in keeping with the spirit of the times. He also simply got tired of making excuses when people asked him, when the information age would finally reach Omega.

No one at Omega knew much about information systems, so they decided to hire a systems analyst who was also a good programmer and proficient in hardware, to select and install the right system for them.

After searching for three months, management decided to hire George, a young expert, who came highly recommended as a "genius".

On his first day of work, George posted a sign on the door of his office, as shown in the picture below.

His door was closed most of the time, so that many people were afraid to go into his office.

George was not satisfied with evaluating a few companies to buy the system. George the genius used a different strategy instead. He picked the best available CPU from one vendor, the best storage devices from another vendor, and various pieces of software from a number of vendors. In the end, he came to the president with all the sales brochures describing the advantages of the various components and recommended assembling a system – crème de la crème.

The company followed George's recommendations and purchased the best components available from the various vendors. George spent his time furiously working to coax all the parts of the system to work together. For nearly three months, George worked on the system day and night. Sometimes he could be seen leaving the office at 9:00 AM, still unshaved, after working through the night. When George finally declared that the system was installed and ready, everyone eagerly anticipated savings, improvements and increase in profits. However, the hoped-for improvements did not materialize.

There were two reasons for this. First, although each of the components was of high quality, they did not work well together. George spent considerable effort coaxing the different components to work together, but the result was not an integrated system. Each of the components was designed to work well with other components of the same vendor, but not necessarily with components of other vendors. Even worse, when the company complained to a vendor that some component did not perform to specifications, he always blamed the other vendors for the poor performance. The vendors all accused each other and the company was always caught in the middle. The company learned the hard way, that they should have bought a complete system from a single vendor, and have a single vendor responsible for the system's performance.

However, this was only part of the company's problems. The bigger disappointment was that George did not communicate well with the managers and did not understand their problems. The managers were afraid to disturb a "genius" at work that was hiding behind closed doors and George was so absorbed with the sophistication of the system he developed, that he had neither the time nor the interest to concern himself with the real problems of the company. The system, which George had spent months implementing and integrating, was so complicated that no one else could understand it. It was a live testimony to George's genius and prowess in programming, but it did very little to solve the company's problems. A much simpler system, geared to the company's problems would have been more helpful. George the genius has forgotten the old principle, "Keep It Simple Stupid" or KISS.

To make matters worse, George made sure that no one in the company would learn how to manage the system. This, he figured, would make him indispensable and therefore his job would be secure. His boss tried to persuade him to teach someone else how to manage the system. He explained that George could never be promoted unless someone else knew his job, but to no avail.

The simple fact is that no one in this world is indispensable, not even the President of the United States. The surest way to be laid-off is to make every one aware that you are indispensable. Your superiors will realize that they have little control over you, since you can always threaten to leave, taking all your secrets with you. No one likes to negotiate from such a position of weakness. They will make all efforts to replace you. This is exactly what happened to George.

While many companies spend time, effort, and money searching in the latest magazine articles and sales brochures for how to maximize their production, or minimize their cost of doing business, they often overlook the most important search a company can make – looking at the problems, at themselves and the condition of their organization. After all, it is pointless to automate a poorly running, less than profitable company. If a company is a mess under a manual system, when it is automated it will become an automated mess. Yet, many companies do this every day.

It has been recently stressed in books and articles that the objective of a company is to make profit not to be efficient. Accounting rules, efficiency studies, management insights, maximization concepts, optimization programs, automation, labor-saving techniques and efficiency for efficiency sake, often stressed by managers and executives, are irrelevant. Only increases in profit, cash-flow and return on investment are important. The only things that affect these directly are increased throughput, leaner inventory and reduced operating expenses.

I recall the case of an engineer from a window-manufacturing company, who proudly showed me a new automated saw that cost twenty thousand dollars. His study proved that the saw operator could cut a window in 60% of the time, achieving a saving of 40%. I asked the engineer if the saw operator could previously cut all the windows the assembly line was able to produce. The engineer said, "Yes." I then asked him if after the labor savings the line would produce more windows. The engineer answered, "Not necessarily. We cannot produce or even sell more windows but we will save 40% of the saw operator's time and it took me only two days to make this survey."

What this really meant was that the saw operator would either slow down his pace in order not to stand idle, or would have more time to smoke and drink coffee, since there was nothing else he could do at his workstation. In either case, the throughput would not increase and the company would not make more money. I suspect that the main reason the study was performed was that this was easy to do.

It would have been a different story if the saw operator could not cut all the windows needed and increasing his production would increase the output of the whole line. This would have been a real saving and a real improvement, because it would have eliminated a bottleneck that was preventing an increase in throughput and profits.

From this example we can learn what companies should do. Instead of seeking to increase the efficiency of a single workstation, they should analyze their total operation, process by process, to increase total throughput.

Ideally, help in analyzing your company objectively should come from outside, because inside managers find it difficult to break down the walls of conventional thinking within which they are confined.

When deciding to apply optimization or integrate a new information system in your organization, consider that you may not be able to take advantage of all the benefits the supplier promises you. After spending huge amounts of money and improving efficiency of a workstation, you may find that your bottom line has not improved, or worse yet, you may have actually become less profitable as explained below.

If a supplier of optimizing equipment promises that his product will reduce the man-hours of labor necessary to produce a part by 50%, that promise is intoxicating. He may even be able to prove it in theory and show you case studies. However, implicit in his promise may be the hidden fact that such a reduction may only be realized if twice as many parts are produced, or if the work force at that station is cut in half. Neither of these actions may be feasible in your case. After all, you may not need twice as many parts because you cannot assemble, ship, or even sell twice as many products. In addition, eliminating 50% of your workforce may disrupt your parts scheduling and labor availability. If you have 3 men working at that station, you will be either short-handed, which will cut down on the number of parts processed, or you will be over-staffed, which will tend to cut down the savings promised.

Even worse though, is when investing in equipment to optimize one workstation not only makes no difference in your company's ability to deliver products and services on a timely and profitable basis, but the cash invested in the equipment and/or software reduces your cash flow, causes the company to pay workers for idle time and actually reduces profits.

This shows us why optimizations and system improvements cannot be viewed in isolation from other considerations. It may be a waste of time and money if the process does not need optimization or automation.

It is important to realize that sometimes, local efficiencies can cause global inefficiencies. This is because nobody works in a vacuum. Everyone is part of the organization. For example, in a production environment, adding a sophisticated system in one stage of the operation may change the character of the entire production process and require changes in layout, production sequence, production scheduling etc.

Here is a two-stage process that can help achieve the increased profit, increased throughput, efficient use of resources, and decreased operating expense you may be looking for:

Stage One - Reviewing your Operation

Carefully review your entire operation. In a production environment, this would include looking at manufacturing processes, material flow, inventory, factory layout, material handling, ordering, shipping, etc. It is important to review these elements in terms of improving final results.

Identify and define the areas presenting the best opportunities for improvement that will increase your throughput, reduce your inventory or reduce your overall operating expenses. Pay special attention to bottlenecks that reduce your throughput.

List and arrange the areas of opportunity in the order of priority that yields the biggest gains with the least investment first.

Stage Two - Improvement Projects

Select the first project from your priority list to implement.

As each project is selected, this is the time to analyze whether optimization or automation will yield better or more cost-effective results than manual improvements. Do not be embarrassed to introduce manual improvements if they are more cost effective just because today it is in vogue to automate everything. Remember the importance of the KISS principle.

Analyze the selected area of improvement to see how it affects all the other areas of opportunity. Does it change the conditions of the next project? If not, proceed to the next project. If so, reanalyze, and reprioritize the remaining opportunities on your list.

The last step is important because it is here where mistakes are made and are often hidden from view. Each process in your organization is interrelated with others. Inefficiencies at one stage may disappear when a prior or subsequent stage is made more efficient. On the other hand, previous efficiencies may disappear when a preceding or succeeding stage is made more productive. The trick is to keep looking for the optimum integration among all your processes.

Moreover, this integration is different for every organization, regardless of your experience in another company, or what the hardware and software suppliers tell you.

This brings us to the need for an outside consultant. Many managers are not able to identify the problems within their company and are not able to suggest or bring about improvements without input from an outsider, because they are used to the status quo. The good manager looks for help from an outside consultant. The poor manager thinks he knows it all. The wisest men in history used outside consultants. The Bible mentions that Moses, the great leader, used an outside consultant, as did King Solomon the wisest of all men. It has been said that you can tell the good U.S. Presidents by the quality of their consultants. So why should a good manager think twice before hiring one?

A consultant will also help you when shopping for equipment and software to improve your bottom line. A good consultant will make sure that you don't just read the sales brochures or operating manuals of the suppliers when buying new equipment or hardware. He will know how to ask the right questions as you review your operations, will help you define the priorities and the areas of opportunity in your company, and assist you in the selection and review of the available courses of action.

When choosing a consultant or an executive for your company, always remember the words of a Swiss MIS director supervising hundred and fifty systems analysts and programmers who was about to retire. An EDP magazine editor asked him: "If you could ask candidates for your position only one question before hiring one of them what would it be?" He answered that the question would be: "When solving a problem what is more important to you: recent technology or business needs? If the man answered, "Recent technology", I would not hire him for any position. If the man answered, "Both recent technology and business needs are important to me", I would hire him as a programmer. If the man answered, "Business needs are more important to me", I would hire him as my replacement.

Chapter 5

Evaluation of Employees Made Simple

Albert: What does your boss do all day?
Simon: Absolutely nothing.
Albert: And what is your job?
Simon: I help him.

– from Henry Ekstein's management briefings

A client once complained to me, that whenever he asks about an employee's performance, the human resources department gives him a thick folder full of tests, evaluation sheets, reviews by superiors and other documents. "In the end, after half an hour of reading, I am confused. I would like to change this cumbersome system. This system may be good for those that have the time and patience to deal with the many details, but I would like to change it and get something simpler. If I wanted more details, I could always use the present system. Could you design a simple method that would let me know at a glance whether the employee was worth keeping?" I promised him that I would try.

Evaluating performance of managers and employees is always a difficult task. As in every evaluation process, it is important to first define the criteria of evaluation and the units of measurement. These criteria may vary from one situation to another and even the same criteria may be assigned different degrees of importance, or different weights, in different situations. Let us explore two criteria that my clients found useful in their performance evaluation process, and a tool that simplifies application of the units of measurement.

Employees often complain about their managers, and always find good reasons to do so. For example, their efforts are not appreciated, or their bonus is too small. However, managers are not far behind, they also complain about their subordinates. The complaints vary from poor performance to disruption of other employees, and include almost every fault you could possibly imagine. It is as if God created antagonistic pairs: landlord and tenant, cat and dog, manager and subordinate.

Perhaps it is helpful to realize that every manager and every employee contributes something positive and useful to the company, but at the same time may cause harm and disruption, because he or she has individual traits and needs that clash with the group. This is true of any two people working or living together. Even in the best marriage, each partner feels occasionally unhappy about what his or her spouse thinks or does.

You might think that any employee who causes some harm or disruption should be let go. However it is not that simple. Even in the best case, adding employees causes some disruption. Take a simple example where a single clerk performs a function. As the company grows, another clerk is hired to help the first. The second clerk increases the capacity of the department, which is a positive contribution. However, he also causes some disruption. He has to be trained which decreases the output of the first clerk. Some time will be spent on coordination of effort between the two, something that was not needed when there was only one clerk. As the number of clerks increases you may need to add a supervisor, which adds to the cost of operation. When you add more clerks, they may decide to join a union, which has some benefits but also creates disruptions. Therefore, assuming no other changes are made in the system other than adding the extra clerks, the output will not increase in proportion to the number of clerks added.

Once you realize, that there is no perfect manager or perfect employee you will be more tolerant of other people's shortcomings. If you have a subordinate who is a good performer but causes you some grief, consider yourself lucky: If you choose not to suffer from a good performer, you may end up suffering from a poor performer.

The only question that you have to ask is whether the harm and grief caused by an employee outweighs his usefulness. A simple matrix, which my clients dubbed Ekstein's Square, may help you in this task. The matrix is easy to construct.

Draw a square and divide it into ten columns. Mark each column with a number from one to ten. Next, divide the square into ten rows and mark each row by a number from one to ten. Let the numbers on the top describe degrees of usefulness of an employee with number one indicating "useless" and number ten indicating "useful". Let the numbers on the left of the square indicate degrees of harmlessness of an employee with number one indicating "harmful" and number ten indicating "harmless". When you are done, you will have a square as shown below.

EKSTEIN'S SQUARE

		Useless					Useful				
		1	2	3	4	5	6	7	8	9	10
Harmful	1										
	2										
	3										
	4										
	5										
	6										
	7										
	8										
	9										
Harmless	10										

The best employee you can hope for is one who is harmless and useful. This is the ideal case. The worst case is an employee who is harmful and useless. If you mark the ratings correctly you will find that rarely will you give a 10 in "useful" or a 10 in "harmless". Most grades will fall between 1 and 10.

Based on these ratings the best employee who is useful and harmless gets an "A" rating. The employee who is useless and harmful gets an "F" rating.

You probably have employees of both kinds in your company. They may not be close to any of the extremes. They are most likely closer to the middle.

The square can be divided into four regions. Region **A** is positive. Ratings in this region have a good combination of usefulness and harmlessness. Here you will find employees who are creative, work hard and create minimum disruptions. Region **F** is negative. Employees in this region are disruptive and of limited usefulness. Region **B** contains employees who contribute a great deal to the company, but do not get along well with others and, therefore cause considerable harm. It is interesting to note that many geniuses belong to this region. Region **C** contains employees who cause minimum disruptions and therefore are harmless, but not very productive. The square and the regions are shown below.

EKSTEIN'S SQUARE

		Useless					Useful				
		1	2	3	4	5	6	7	8	9	10
Harmful	1										
	2										
	3			F					B		
	4			WORST					AVERAGE		
	5										
Harmless	6										
	7										
	8			C					A		
	9			AVERAGE					BEST		
	10										

The square is not enough to give a detailed evaluation of an employee's performance. It serves mainly as a simple tool for fast comparison of employees and to evaluate whether an employee causes more problems than his contributions are worth.

To get more accurate results, make copies of the square and ask a number of executives to evaluate the same employee as objectively as they can. Compare the results obtained by different executives and adjust results to compensate for personal prejudice.

Chapter 6

The Sisyphus Principle

Greek mythology offers a lesson for manufacturing efficiency

When I was studying Greek mythology, my professor discussed the story of Sisyphus the King of Corinth, who as punishment for his evil reign, was condemned by the gods to an eternity of rolling a huge stone up-hill, which would always fall back down before he could reach the top.

A student questioned the professor about such a punishment. When compared to burning in hell, or having your eyes gouged out, or some of the other awful things the gods would mete out to the condemned, pushing a stone up-hill didn't seem so bad.

The professor explained that the punishment was not physical pain, but mental torment – the torment of working so hard, yet being completely unproductive.

I have always wondered what message Sisyphus has for our generation. After observing many work environments, it occurred to me that Sisyphus was actually condemned to handling materials eternally without producing anything of value. You can still find Sisyphus in many companies today, in the form of workers handling materials, toiling hard, and producing no value for their customers.

These workers may or may not be frustrated. After all they are being paid. Most of them may not even know that they are completely unproductive, because they are tired at the end of the day and everyone is doing what the boss tells them to do. The truth is that this non-productive effort shows up in the cost of labor and in the bottom line of the company, not in the psyche of the worker.

To increase profits, a company may raise prices, lower costs or increase productivity. In today's competitive market, raising prices is too risky for most businesses, and lowering costs is equally difficult. This leaves us with increasing productivity, which is not always easy but is usually possible.

Most attempts to increase productivity involve incentives, additional training, new equipment or other capital-intensive methods. There is one approach though, that is often overlooked. It involves the one variable that greatly influences productivity in a production environment: Reduction of material handling through better plant and workstation layout.

Numerous studies have shown that up to 75% of man-hours in manufacturing is consumed by material handling. No matter how automated a process is, the materials must move from station to station until the product is complete. Moreover, the component materials must be received, stored and brought to the workstations on time in the right quantity, and the completed product must be moved from the final assembly to shipping. In addition, there is waste product to be removed and disposed of in an orderly fashion. In today's automated and optimized workplace, it seems unreasonable that there would be any inefficient workers. Yet, no matter how automated the production process is, material handling is everywhere and Sisyphus is doing too much of it.

What I have found over the years is that even though a factory becomes increasingly automated, the basic plant layout stays the same for a long time – 5, 10 and even 20 years. Most manufacturing companies and assemblers of the various products make automation their first priority, and all too often make layout their last priority. Certainly, they consider layout, but usually they do not seek a custom layout designed to minimize material handling inefficiencies particular to their operation.

When automated equipment is added, the department or workstation may have a new layout, but its relation to the rest of the manufacturing process is not reanalyzed, and material handling and bottlenecks up or down the line all too often rob the manufacturer of the savings offered by the new equipment.

Those manufacturers who know they need a complete and integrated plant layout, approach it all too often in the wrong way. The two most common mistakes are:

1. Using in-house managers and supervisors to design the layout

2. Accepting the offer of material or equipment suppliers to provide the layout free of charge.

In-house management and supervisors are usually under too much pressure running their own departments and have no patience to design layouts. In addition, it is difficult for them to be objective. They are reluctant to admit that the previous layout they designed is no longer appropriate. Even if they want to design a new layout, they do not have the time, education and experience to do it well. They end up planning a layout during lunch over their coffee and cake.

The problem with materials or equipment suppliers arises because they usually design one basic layout and try to make it fit each facility, in the spirit of "one size fits all."

The best solution is to consult with an expert, inside or outside the company, who will help you lay out your production facility as an integrated cohesive unit.

Unless you are an expert, poor layout is hard to spot when all your workers are busy 100% of the time. If there are no apparent bottlenecks, and no one is standing idly waiting for work to arrive from another department or workstation, it will appear that production is running smoothly, and everyone will be pleased. However, when we think of Sisyphus, maybe too many of the busy workers are really pushing stones uphill only to have them fall back before they reach the top. Maybe if the curse were lifted, they would reach the top making their jobs more meaningful and your profits more plentiful.

Here are five steps you can take to remove the curse of Sisyphus from your plant:

• Realize that plant layout is an important variable that controls your plant's productivity regardless of optimization or automation.

• Set a goal to redesign your production layout and material flow with the objectives being to reduce material handling to a minimum, optimize the space for each operation, and do it all at an optimal cost.

• Begin work with an external or internal consultant on these improvements. While there are dozens of possible layouts, there are usually 10 to 12 simple, feasible layout options for every case. Any one of these can save you money by removing five to ten percent of the unnecessary and unproductive material handling. One or two of these may save you up to twenty percent. These layouts you cannot afford to miss.

• If no one in your company is competent to design layouts, avoid designing your own layouts. In the short term, it may seem the least expensive way to arrange your factory. In the long term, it will cost you more than you might have spent for a good consultant. If a consultant designs a layout that helps you save five percent more on material handling, the resulting savings over a five-year period makes hiring a professional well-worth the extra cost.

• Avoid hiring a consultant who will give you just one or two layouts. This consultant may quote you a lower price, but you need a variety of options to be sure you don't miss the one or two better options. Additionally, your managers and foremen are unlikely to implement any changes willingly. By having many options, you can enlist their assistance in making the final decisions using the Pairing of Options principle, and by doing so earn their enthusiastic consent and support.

Here are the three stages of planning an effective layout:

1. Allocate space to the different departments. When choosing locations for each department, place those departments that you expect to grow where future expansion is possible. In each case, consider also the cost and benefit of allocating some extra space for future expansion.

2. Design a block layout. Divide the total facility into blocks, one block for each department according to the allocated number of square feet in step one. The departments should be positioned in a way that minimizes material handling. You may want to design ten different block layouts and then develop number eleven, better than the ten, using the "Pairing of Options" principle.

3. Design a layout for each department. Each department is laid out in the block allocated to it in the block layout. Here, too, you will probably want to design a number of layouts for each department and develop a better layout using the "Pairing of Options" method.

In stage 3, you may find that you allocated too little or too much space to some departments. In this case, go back to stage 1.

It is essential to involve all managers and supervisors in all stages and make them partners to the effort. This way, they will be glad to cooperate and will implement the layout willingly.

Chapter 7

The Matchmaker's Principle

Success is the ability to go from one failure to another with no loss of enthusiasm.

— Sir Winston Churchill

Eager to get the best of the crop, Mr. White, the president of an office supply company, rushed to the campus early in March to recruit new graduates. Mr. White thought that to succeed, each new employee must have the potential to become one day the president of the company.

Five of the new graduates were placed in sales. Their job was to visit customers and offer them office supplies, customized printed forms and other related items. This took place before the days that there were super stores like Staples and Office Depot.

Mr. White had lunch with his friend, a president of a company who was my client, and told him about his problems: The new trainees did not work out very well. Some of them did not bring enough sales to justify their salary, but Mr. White was not yet ready to lay-off any of them. His friend suggested that he talk to me about the situation to see whether I could help.

I told Mr. White that I was neither a sales nor a marketing specialist, and therefore I could not guarantee results. Mr. White said that I should try anyway. He was willing to take the risk.

They introduced me to Johnny the worst salesman of the group. My first impression of him was very poor. His suit was too small for him. The sleeves were too short; the pants showed too much of his socks. His suit looked like a teenager's suit worn by an adult. His tie must have seen better times. His briefcase was probably inherited from his father or grandfather. I said to myself that if I needed office supplies I would not want to buy them from Johnny. Nevertheless, during my first conversation with him I changed my mind. I found him to be an extremely intelligent man.

I asked Johnny to tell me how he spent his workday. He was quite candid with me. He told me that he started knocking on doors at nine in the morning. Sometimes by eleven thirty, he got all the rejections he could take, so he took an early lunch. Often he took a two-hour lunch and occasionally he would not return to work in the afternoon because he simply could not take any more rejections, and because it made little difference anyway, "Nobody wants to buy from me." he explained.

I asked him if he sold anything at all. He said that he did sell on occasion, but it was far from enough. I kept probing, "Are you courteous to those who choose not buy from you?"

He said, "Well, most of the time, but sometimes I am so frustrated by their lack of courtesy that I am anxious to leave."

He trusted me, because we agreed in the beginning that whatever we discussed would be strictly confidential.

I had the impression that he viewed the customer as an enemy, as the source of all his aggravations. That is why he took long lunches. He tried to minimize his contact with the enemy. I noticed this when he said, "Nobody wants to buy from me." This also implied that he believed that something was wrong with him as a salesman. I reasoned that in order to become a good salesman, he must change both his perception of the customer as his enemy, and his perception of himself as a poor salesman. I believed that with proper training and motivation there was a good chance that Johnny could become a productive salesman.

I said to him, "I am willing to help you. But first I will tell you a story." He was frustrated by the whole situation, and was willing to listen to anything that might help. This is the story I told him.

"The Hebrew sages of old believed that forty days before a child was born, it was decreed in heaven who would be his or her match. All that was needed was to find the predestined one in order to be happy. Not only was the right match predestined, also predestined were all the dates that a person had to meet before he or she would find the chosen one. Therefore, the Hebrew sages never refused a matchmaker, no matter how unrealistic the match looked to them, and no matter the difference of social strata. They believed that this was either their match or one of the dates that would bring them one step closer to their predestined one. Following the matchmaker's principle, they went on all the dates, until they met the predestined one and were married."

"Johnny, I want you to believe that it has been predestined in heaven who will buy from you, and also who will not buy from you. Moreover, you cannot get to those who will buy from you, unless you first visit those that will refuse to buy from you. Therefore, if someone buys from you thank him profusely; he has helped you make money. If someone refuses to buy from you, also thank him profusely; he has done you a big favor. He brought you one step closer to the one who will buy from you. Follow the matchmaker's principle. Follow it and you will succeed."

Johnny was visibly upset. "I am not a religious man. I do not even believe in a superior being. Do you really expect me to believe that it is predestined who will buy from me? That's pure nonsense. How am I going to succeed using a theory I don't believe to be true?"

I was taken aback by his strong objection. After a few moments I said, "Who told you that a theory has to be true in order to be useful and produce results? In fact, we do not know if any of our theories are 100% true. Take for example the principles of Newtonian mechanics that the mass of a body is a fixed quantity, and that time and space have absolute dimensions. The theory of relativity proved that these principles were not true. Despite that, assuming that these theories were true helped engineers to develop the steam engine, the automobile, the airplane and many other useful things. The same is true in chemistry and other sciences. So why would you want to use only true theories that may not even exist? Assume that what I told you is true, and you will see good results even if the theory is not true."

It took me a while to persuade Johnny, but I soon found that he was so desperate that he was willing to try almost anything. I explained to him that if he believed in my theory then every prospect was a friend, even the one that did not buy. They should all be treated with courtesy and a smile.

I looked at Johnny and the sore state of his appearance, and told him that this was not a way to visit customers. I suggested that he invest a few hundred dollars in his future. He needed the money to buy a new suit, shoes, a few ties, a few shirts and a new briefcase. I asked him to see me on the following day in his new attire, before he went to see customers.

When Johnny came to see me the next morning, I could not believe my eyes. He seemed to be a different man. He looked fresh, well groomed and well dressed. He said, "I asked my mother to come with me to the store and pick the most appropriate suit and matching ties, shirts and shoes." Indeed everything he wore was well coordinated. Apparently, his mother had good taste.

Now we were ready to start. I helped Johnny design an appointment log. He had to plan his appointments in a way that minimizes travel time and maximizes the number of appointments. He had tried to do it before, but there was room for improvement. We also expanded his log a bit to make room for recording each appointment in detail.

The things we wanted to know about each visit were:

1. Date and time
2. Company address
3. Telephone number
4. Name of person seen
5. Did he buy?
6. If he did not buy, reason for not buying
7. When to visit him again

We agreed that we would meet every day after work, review the appointment log and decide what to do the following day.

The next day Johnny did not make any sales. He was sad and insecure. He asked me how he would make a living if there were no sales. I told him, "You have to live by the "Fisherman's principle."

"What does that mean," asked Johnny.

I explained to him that the fisherman goes to sea not knowing for sure that he will catch any fish. Is it possible that he will find no fish today? Of course it is. However, if he goes to sea every day, he will eventually find enough fish to feed himself and his family. I told him, "You are like this fisherman. Have patience. Do your job diligently and you will build up sales in time. Success is built gradually, just like a bricklayer builds a big house – one brick at a time."

We found two incomplete entries in the log. The reason was that Johnny filled out the log partially from memory during his lunch break, using the customers' business cards, which I had told him to ask for. However, some customers did not have business cards with them. Johnny could not complete the log, because he forgot the details. We agreed that in the future, he would fill out the log immediately after the interview.

While there were no sales the first day, two customers agreed to see him again, one in three weeks to order stationery and one in four weeks to order business forms. We designed a tickler file and filed the business cards of the two customers in the proper places.

I made sure that Johnny would treat each customer as a friend, whether or not he bought from him. I also stressed that it is important to check whether the customer had any problems and help him solve them. The best salesmen are those that come to the customer to offer solutions, rather than to sell merchandise.

"Finally", I said to him, "do not forget to ask the customer for names of friends and associates that you could also help."

The first week was not great. The second week was better. I tried to help Johnny look at each prospect as a challenge, "Find out what makes him tick." Johnny was intelligent and soon got the hang of it. You could see his progress from week to week.

He built up his confidence gradually. When he looked in the mirror, he saw a nice well-groomed man. The customers who belittled him when his appearance was poor treated him now with respect. He slowly changed his perception of the customers and his perception of himself.

After only four months, Johnny was number three in sales in a company of twelve salesmen. The last words I heard from him, before I left after finishing my project, were "Changing my perceptions of myself and of the customers has changed my performance and you helped me change my perceptions."

Chapter 8

The "Hook in the Wall" Principle

Don't be misled by your eyes.
— *based on Numbers 15:39*

Kaiser Wilhelm of Germany announced he intended to visit Mecklenburg, a region known for its large, world-famous Belgian Horses. If you've ever visited Disneyland, you might have seen Belgian Horses. Each of these horses stands about seven feet high. They were used in Europe to transport heavy loads.

In honor of the Kaiser's visit, the region's councilmen thought they should prepare a ceremony befitting the Emperor of Germany. Knowing the Kaiser was a science buff who liked horses, they thought they would prepare a treat for him.

On the day of the Kaiser's visit, they joined two perfectly fitting hollow hemispheres, two feet in diameter. They pumped out all the air inside, and the resulting vacuum served to hold the two hemispheres together. They attached two huge Belgian horses, one to each hemisphere, trying to pull the hemispheres apart. Pull as they might, the hollow hemispheres remained joined.

The Kaiser asked the councilmen to add another horse to each side. Now two horses were hooked on each side, and they too, were unable to separate the hemispheres. The Kaiser asked them to continue to increase the number of horses until there were seven on each side, for a total of 14 horses. Surprisingly, The hemispheres still remained joined. The Kaiser was amazed and could not believe his eyes. He clearly enjoyed the show.

The famous author, Yakov Perelman, read of this demonstration and was perplexed. He could not understand how such force did not pull the two hemispheres apart. He decided to measure the force. In any case, it would be interesting to see how much force the hemispheres had withstood.

In his book "Interesting Mechanics" he wrote that he first measured the force when two horses pulled, one on each side. The force was one horsepower[*]. He then measured the force with four horses pulling, two horses on each side. The

---

[*] By horsepower, I refer to the force a single horse can exert by pulling.

measurement showed slightly more than 1.4 horsepower. When there were five horses on each side, the force increased slightly. When there were seven horses on each side the force was still greater, but no matter how many horses he placed on both sides, the force never reached two horsepower.

These results were equally mystifying. How could having one horse on each side only result in one horsepower of force? Moreover, how could increasing the amount of horses to seven on each side not increase the force beyond two horsepower? Mr. Perelman concluded that the horses on one side held the hemispheres, while the horses on the other side actually produced the force that attempted to pull them apart. Replacing the horses on one side with a hook in a wall would not change the resulting force at all.

He also observed that, adding horses just added confusion since not all horses would pull at the same time and the same direction to produce an additive force. Some horses pulled forward, some backwards, some pulled to the left, others to the right. As a result, they produced a smaller net force.

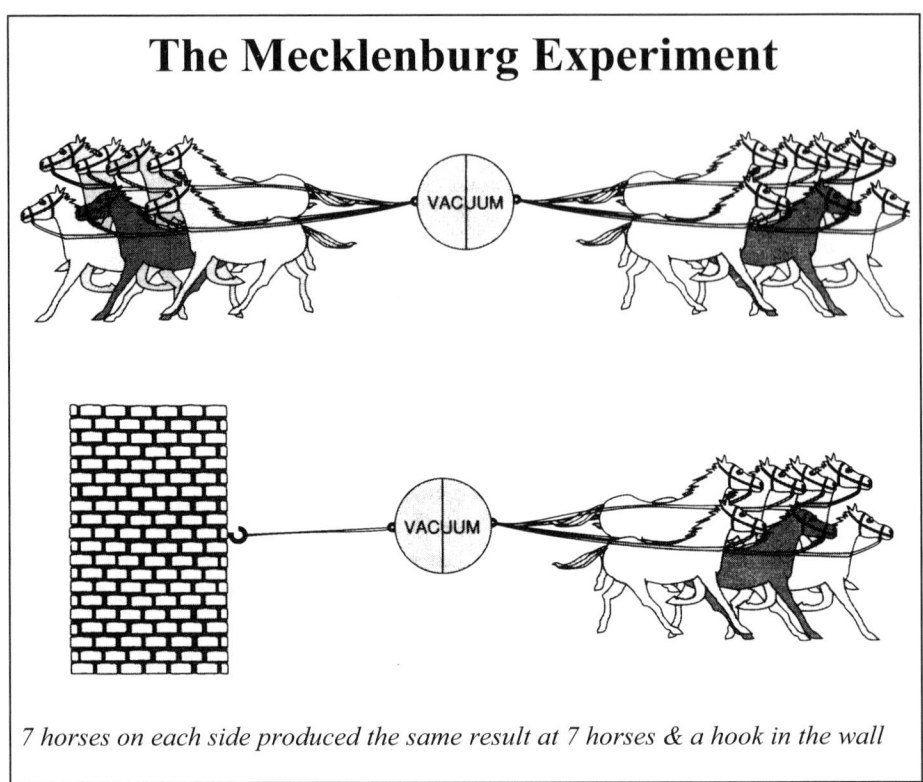

7 horses on each side produced the same result at 7 horses & a hook in the wall

This story has always fascinated me because it taught me a few valuable lessons in analyzing how some people try to solve management problems in their businesses.

Surprisingly, what you see could be misleading. The Kaiser and all the people present saw fourteen horses pulling. However, in reality the pulling force was less than that of two horses!

There are many other examples proving that what you see is not necessarily what is there. Just walk outdoors on a clear, moonless evening and look at the beautiful skies studded with thousands of stars. Did you ever consider that of all the beautiful stars you see not even one is really where you see it? Some might not even exist anymore. The reason is simple. If a star is five thousand light years away, the light the star emits travels five thousand years to reach your eyes. What you see is where the star was five thousand years ago. By now the star could be billions of miles away. It might have exploded or might have been sucked in by a black hole thousands of years ago, yet your eyes see the star as if it were there. In reality the place where you see the star is dark, empty outer space. This is true of every single star you see. What you see as beautiful star-studded skies is just an illusion, a grand spectacle in outer space masquerading as substance. These examples may help you avoid being misled by your eyes when you observe what is happening around you in personal life and in the workplace.

Imagine yourself visiting an office for the first time. You might see busy employees making copies on Xerox machines, talking on the phone, working hard at computer screens, leading you to believe that they produce optimum results. But is this really so or is it just an illusion? Are they doing the right things? Are their efforts producing maximum value to the customer? After all, what is really important is not hard work but positive results.

Could the office be similar to the example of fourteen horses? As you recall, the seven horses on one side, even though they worked hard, produced no results at all. They just kept the hemispheres in place like a "hook in the wall". Without them the other seven horses would have walked away taking the two hemispheres with them.

Remember the "Hook in the Wall" principle when improving your operation. For example, if you work in a factory that employs laborers to screw caps on bottles by hand, and you need to increase the output, the natural tendency would be to hire more people. However, employing more workers might not be the solution.

If each person needs two hands to screw tops on the bottles, usually one is to hold the bottle, and the other screws on the cap. Perhaps if you were able to find a stationary holder for the bottles, "a hook in the wall", one worker could screw-on a cap with each hand and almost double the output with little increase in labor cost.

More people, more money and more equipment do not always produce more results. Just as Yakov Perelman discovered, after the first two horses, any increase in animals resulted in a marginal increase in force. The same is true of employees. New employees require the valuable time of more experienced employees to train them and they require more management attention. They often reduce the level of quality, produce more scrap and may adversely affect customer satisfaction. These factors, together with the slower pace of trainees, increase expenses and may increase the output only marginally.

I recall a case from a telecommunications company. Management kept adding customer service representatives to reduce caller's waiting time. At one point, they employed 160 customer service representatives and the average waiting time of callers was still 11.5 minutes. Management urged the director of customer service to hire more people to reduce the waiting time. Instead, the director asked me to assist him and using the "hook in the wall" approach, we reduced the waiting time to 1.5 minutes, while simultaneously trimming the staff to 72 employees. In the process, he saved the company close to three million dollars in yearly payroll and benefits. It is interesting to note that in this case, due to high turnover, not even one customer service representative was laid-off. Attrition and transfers to other departments reduced the staff.

Next time you need an increase in output, be creative in your analysis. Resist the easy solution of hiring more people, working longer shifts or getting more machines. We know those tactics do not always produce the desired results, and a better solution might be just hanging on the wall.

What we have demonstrated in this chapter is that adding more of the same, like horses or employees, yields diminishing returns. The same is true of other production factors. Take space for example. We often tend to complain that we do not have enough space and that is why productivity is low. It is possible that if you added some space productivity would increase. However, if you add too much space you will soon find that office employees must walk farther to see the clerks they need. If you work in a production environment, the material handlers will have to walk longer stretches to transfer goods between workstations, deliver raw materials to the production area or transfer finished goods to the warehouse. All of these factors reduce productivity.

You may find this principle to be true even in your kitchen. If your kitchen is too small, it may not be comfortable to prepare in it large meals and you may want to enlarge your kitchen. Most people I know love large kitchens. Remember though, that making your kitchen larger increases the distance from the counter to the refrigerator, from the counter to the stove and from the refrigerator and the stove to the dining table. Owners of large kitchens spend more time on food preparation walking from one work center to the other, than owners of smaller kitchens. As a result they are more tired. This does not mean that you should necessarily settle for a small kitchen, just that you should be aware of the trade-offs when you make your decision. In any event, if you have a small kitchen, take heart, it is not all bad; you are saving valuable time and energy every day.

The same is true of capital. Spending too little is not good, but spending too much may not cure the problem either. In the United State we tend to throw money at problems to make them go away. Our public education is a good example. Public education in the United Stated is in a poor state even though we spend much more to educate a child enrolled in a public school than parochial schools do. Parochial schools are able to spend much less money per child and get much better results. The real solution to improving public education probably requires generating more motivation on part of children and parents, and having parents more involved in what is going on in their children's schools.

For example, an investigation by "Sixty Minutes" showed that schools for children of parents serving in the armed forces rank among the best in the country. They also boast the highest achievements in school integration, with a lower cost per student. This is achieved mainly through strong parent involvement in daily operation of the schools, both inside and outside the classroom.

Surprisingly, in a majority of schools parental involvement in classroom operation is discouraged. Moreover, often young teachers see parents involvement as a blatant intrusion, to be avoided whenever possible.

The majority of teachers and parents think that increasing the school budget will solve the problem. Unfortunately, this is not the case.

This example may seem remote from what we have discussed at the beginning of this chapter. However, in reality, it is just another case of finding creative solutions – of "Finding a Hook in the Wall". This powerful principle applies to nearly everything we do.

Chapter 9

A Matter of Faith

I'm not a teacher, only a fellow traveler of whom you asked the way. I pointed ahead — ahead of myself as well as you.

— George Bernard Shaw

One evening I received a call from a man who introduced himself as Victor Brown. He said that he had spoken with a client of mine, who thought that I could help him solve his problem.

When I asked him what his problem was, he told me that he owned a two hundred eighty employees company that produced windows. The company made a small profit each year. To increase profits, he hired a consultant who spent two years in the plant timing every operation. The consultant finished his job and gave him a thick report showing that the employees work only 60% of the time. If productivity could be increased to only 80%, the yearly savings on labor would amount to over one million dollars, which would substantially improve profits.

When the plant manager and supervisors were confronted with the report, they were furious and threatened to quit. The consultant was afraid that the supervisors would do him bodily harm, and did not even show up to collect his last week's fee.

Victor thought that he had persuaded the managers not to quit, but a business associate had told him that he had received resumes in the mail from two of Victor's managers. Victor was afraid that he would not only lose the expected savings but also the plant management.

I explained to Victor that he should have called me two years ago, and that now might be too late. Victor did not give up, though. He insisted that I visit for at least a few days and charge him for the time, even if nothing could be done. I warned him that I could not promise him anything, but if he wanted, I would come, out of respect for my client who recommended me.

Next day I visited the plant. When I approached Ludwig, the plant manager, he said he had no time to talk to me. I invited him for lunch, but he was not interested. I had the feeling, however, that the man wanted to talk to somebody about the injustice that had been done to him, to the supervisors and to the workers, but that nobody wanted to listen. I therefore tried a different approach.

"I heard the story from the president. I never make judgments after hearing only one side. I would now like to hear what you have to say. Would you like to tell me your side of the story over lunch?"

"What's the point?" answered Ludwig. "You are just another consultant. We know that the president brought you here to confirm the findings of the first consultant."

"Nothing could be further from truth." I said. "I am not a consultant. I have my own methods. I believe that the plant manager and the supervisors should determine the current level of productivity, not someone from the outside. The most I can do is show you the way."

"Would you accept our findings even if we showed that productivity was 100%?"

"Yes" I answered, "But first we would have to establish the method that you and your supervisors would use to arrive at the conclusions."

"But we have no time to do it, and our men do not know how to do time studies".

"No problem." I answered. "I can suggest a simple way to do it without time studies, that will take only three minutes a day. But first let me hear your side of the story".

Over lunch, Ludwig opened up. He told me that the consultant timed each operation with a stopwatch. He was "breathing down the neck" of the operators, who complained bitterly to the supervisors that they could not work that way. In the end he concluded from his time studies, that what now took 100 minutes could be done in 60 minutes, actually meaning that the supervisors and employees gave only 60% of effort.

"Did the consultant show you how to get from 100 minutes to 60?"

"No. He did not. He just said that things should be rearranged. The layout should be changed. I suspect that he was preparing another project for himself. He probably wanted to spend here another two years. Let me tell you, we are not dancing here. My people work hard. In the evening we are all tired. We give 100% of effort but no one appreciates it. I told the president that if we worked at 60% as the consultant claimed, then he was welcome to hire the consultant instead of me. Maybe he could do a better job. I was so disgusted that I was ready to quit."

"I am not surprised that you were upset. I would feel the same way in your place, and I am going to say so to the president. I will also explain to him, that to make things work right, you and the supervisors will have to establish the level of productivity, and I will be the first to accept your findings. If the president agrees to these conditions, I will accept the assignment. If not, you will not see me here tomorrow."

Ludwig felt much better. He needed someone to talk to, and needed to get the frustration off his chest. He was also pleased that I agreed with him and that if I were in his place I would be upset too. He said that he was willing to give me a chance, but if the other consultant came back, he would quit.

When I told the president what I said to Ludwig, he was skeptical at first. He did not know whether to continue working with me or not. I helped him analyze his options. In the end he realized that there was a possibility that I could help him, and since this looked like the best option available to him he decided to sign an agreement with me.

I explained to Ludwig and his supervisors that first we must find out how we spend the eight hours of work time. I helped them design a simple sampling sheet the size of small notebook that could fit into a shirt pocket. The sheet included one row for each of the most frequently encountered elements, which we could think of, and had one row for "other" elements not listed on the sheet, as shown on the next page.

I described the sampling procedure to Ludwig and the supervisors. Every time the observer decided to take a reading, he lowered his eyes first and looked at the floor. Then for a split second, he raised his eyes to make the observation and then lowered his eyes again. I called it the photographic observation, because the eyes took a split second picture like a camera. The observer marked a tally stroke on the sheet for each man he saw during the split second. The fifth tally stroke was made horizontally across the previous four, for ease of counting.

Observer: Frank Oliver **Date:** 12 Dec	
Working	
Handling	
Walking	
Reading order	
Talking	
Other	
Remarks	

For example if the observer saw three men, two of them working and one handling, he would make two tally strokes in the "working" row and one tally stroke in the "handling" row. The observation and notation should take about five seconds. Each observer should make about 30 observations a day at random time intervals. This would take about two and a half minutes a day from each supervisor.

At the end of the day, each supervisor would give his sheet to Ludwig who would summarize the readings on each man's monthly summary sheet. The summary sheet had the same rows as the sampling sheet but had twenty-three columns one for each day of the month. If on Monday John made 15 tally strokes in the "working" row, then on his summary sheet Ludwig wrote 15 in the Monday column where it intersected with the "working" row.

At the end of the month there would be a few thousands readings made by the group. These readings would be summarized on one monthly group sheet which would show how many readings of the "working" element were made by the group, how many of the "handling" element and so on. In the end, the total number of readings was summarized and the percentage of readings of each element was calculated. For example if there were in total 10,000 tally strokes and 7000 "working" tally strokes, then the statistical theory as well as plain common sense dictated that employees were working approximately 70% of time during the observation period. The plant management team agreed that this was true.

In reality, things were a little more complex. For example you could find subjective differences between observers: Some would post "work" readings for elements that other would post "handling", and so on. Therefore, I also took my own readings for the sake of comparison. It was also important to define each category precisely. For these reasons it is best to hire a consultant to help conduct such a survey.

In the beginning, Ludwig and the supervisors were a little unsure if they could do it. However, after a little practice they became more confident. They decided who would do the daily summaries on the monthly sheet, who would do the final calculations, and who would store the daily sampling sheets for future reference in case of doubt.

Ludwig and I also took readings, to make sure that the readings of others were not too subjective. Ludwig was also responsible for writing the final report based on the results of the study.

The study took about six weeks to complete. In the end, Ludwig wrote a draft of the final report with my help. The supervisors were told that they could make any corrections to the draft, because the project was theirs and Ludwig's, and that their names would appear on the cover sheet of the report. My name appeared at the bottom.

When the report was ready, it was impressive. We decided that I would go with Ludwig, when he presented the report to the president.

As we walked in, Ludwig proudly presented a copy of the report to the president and told him that he and the supervisors had made the study with my help. Ludwig explained that the study proved that the previous consultant was wrong. The people on the floor worked hard probably giving 80% of effort not 60% as the consultant said. On the other hand, the people worked hard at the wrong things. Only 53% of the time was spent on useful work, producing value to customers. Actually, the work done presently in 100 minutes could be done in 53 minutes by concentrating efforts on the right things.

The president could not believe his ears. He asked me later how it was possible that the same people, who were insulted and wanted to quit when the previous consultant said that what now takes 100 minutes could be done in 60 minutes, were now saying proudly that the consultant was wrong, the same work could be done in just 53 minutes.

I explained to the president that this is the power of my interactive consulting method. It helps managers arrive at conclusions on their own. If you are asked to accept someone else's findings and do not like them, you can be angry and reject his findings. However, if you yourself arrive at the same findings, whom can you blame?

I also explained to the president what I had already clarified to plant management, that there is a difference between efficiency and productivity. Efficiency means doing things right, minimizing use of resources. Productivity means doing the right things. Concentrating on productivity by eliminating all non-productive elements like handling, walking, talking to supervisors to clarify confusing order papers, and the like, would permit employees to spend more time on elements producing value to customers, which is the only important thing. Efficiency comes later. What Ludwig was saying is that the work pace was about 80%, but productivity was only 53%.

The handling and walking elements require some explanation. When a worker is handling finished products, moving them to the shipping department, 500 feet away, he must later walk the same distance back to the department. On his way to the shipping department, he is handling materials. However on the way back he is walking. Hence, by eliminating a handling element you also eliminate a walking element, both of which require effort on the part of the worker but do not produce value to the customer and, therefore, are not productive.

Try to eliminate as many handling elements as you can. A British study has found that time spent on handling and walking elements, including handling of work at the workstation, constitutes up to 75% of total work time.

We eliminated many of the non-productive elements. This enabled the same number of employees to increase output and reduce the cost of labor. The lower prices helped increase sales to the point that new employees were hired. Profit increased and part of the profit was invested in new equipment to further increase productivity and in bonuses to deserving managers and employees.

I worked with this company on few more projects and helped some managers develop their skills and be promoted. The managers had full faith in me and often they were the ones who initiated new projects. They were the ones who asked the president to send me to assist them.

Ironically, the same people that said they had no faith in consultants became my strongest supporters, maybe because I am not a consultant at all. I do not do what consultants do: I do not write reports, I do not make recommendations and I do not tell people what to do.

Chapter 10

The Sexton's Principle

> Successful innovators recognize that discovery of great ideas comes from looking at the same thing as everyone else and observing something different.
> — *Reed Markham*

Some years ago, I worked for a prestigious consulting company. I had just finished an assignment and was waiting to start on a new project. My boss called me to his office to review the new assignment with me.

My boss explained that if I succeeded in the new assignment this would be a real feather in my cap. A number of industrial engineers had already worked on this particular operation and could not make substantial improvements. He said that he hoped that I would have better luck and would complete this assignment shining like a star.

He said all this in order to motivate me. My interpretation, however, was just the opposite. I felt like he was sending me to Siberia for hard labor where neither I nor anyone else could succeed, but I had no choice. I had to go where my company needed me.

The place my boss sent me was an open seaport, built in waters too shallow for ships to dock. Instead, the ships were anchored in deeper waters at some distance from the shore and cargo was unloaded in open sea into barges sent from the port. The barges brought the goods to the port and were unloaded in the shallow waters, which were deep enough for a barge. The ships had to be unloaded quickly. In case of delays, the port had to reimburse the ship owners for lost time.

The port had over a hundred barges. The problem was that the maintenance of the barges was very costly and time consuming. Worse than that though, the maintenance was not very effective. A barge stayed in service only a few years and had to be replaced. As a result, a number of new barges had to be purchased every year.

The port maintenance department was responsible for maintenance of the barges and of all other port equipment. This department employed over 200 employees.

I invited Joe, the department manager, to lunch and asked him to describe the maintenance of a barge. By way of introduction, he explained to me that he would like to do maintenance work on a barge more frequently but since he was short-handed, the maintenance was done less often.

I learned from Joe that maintenance of a barge was a labor-intensive operation that included a number of steps.

First, the barge was pulled by crane from the water and placed on two wooden horses. When the barge was resting on the wooden horses, you could clearly see the "beard" of sea grasses covering its sides and bottom.

The next operation was "shaving the beard" This was done manually using special sharp tools. After the "beard" was gone, you could see the rust. Removing the rust or "chipping" was a difficult and time-consuming operation. The chipping was done manually, by a number of employees, using mallets. The whole barge vibrated. The employees were exposed to sound reverberations that they could not endure for more than fifteen minutes at a time. After fifteen minutes of chipping the workers took a ten-minute break. When it was hot outside, conditions were even worse. The metal barge was hot and the workers choked on the dust released by chipping the rust. The workers got free cold drinks. They drank a lot and went often to the men's room. It was difficult to find employees willing to do the job. They tried higher hourly wages and shorter hours, but most people tired quickly and asked to be transferred.

After the chipping was complete, they looked for holes made by the chipping, in places that the barge was rusted through.

The next operation was welding patches to cover the holes. The patch was usually much larger than the hole, because the metal next to the hole was too thin for welding.

After welding, the next operation was grinding the new welds to blend smoothly into the barge. After grinding, the barge was ready for painting. They painted the barge with rust-preventing paint and then with two more coats of paint. When the paint dried, the barge looked like new and was lowered back into the sea.

I asked Joe to tell me how many man-days each element took. Joe had accurate time records from the past and gave the following times per barge:

Task	Man-days
Lifting barge out of sea and securing it on saw horses	0.5
Shaving the beard	1.0
Chipping	86.0
Welding and grinding	11.0
Painting (3 coats of paint inside and out)	3.0
Lowering barge into sea	0.5
Total man-days	**102.0**

I asked Joe how often the maintenance was done and he said, "Approximately once in fifteen months".

"And how often would you like to do it?" I asked.

"It is not a matter of my desires. We go by the book. We had a consultant here who was an expert on barge maintenance. He wrote a report of about 200 pages. This is our bible, our holy book. In this report, the consultant recommended that we maintain the barges once a year. I would like to do it, but I am so short-handed that I cannot do a lot of thing that need to be done. I asked for more help. The answer was: 'There is no budget, do the best with what you have.' This is a shortsighted policy and in the end, it will cost us more. But what can I do?"

I wanted to become acquainted with the operation, so I went to see it for myself. The truth is that I had a hard time withstanding the vibrations the heat and the dust. They really had sent me to "Siberia".

I tried all kind of ideas to improve the operation and lower the costs. The most time-consuming and most expensive element was chipping. It, therefore, made sense to start with this element. I tried chipping with two mallets one in each hand, but the noise was too great and the workers rebelled at this idea. I tried changing the work and break cycles, but nothing seemed to work.

Joe tried to be helpful. He gave me a copy of the consultant's report. He also told me confidentially that some supervisors said to him: "Henry may be a great engineer and a superior consultant. But he is an amateur when it comes to barges. Why does he try to improve things which he does not understand"?

In the meantime, three weeks passed. I did not sleep well at night. I lost my appetite. I am not the kind of person that goes back to his boss and says, "Sorry, but I could not improve anything." To me an assignment is a personal challenge. I usually do not let go of it until I find something important to improve.

One evening I went out with my friend, and he sensed right away that something was disturbing me. He asked me what the problem was, and I explained to him my predicament. He said to me, "Stop worrying. You will think of something when you least expect it – maybe at night, maybe at a restaurant or the theater. Worry will get you nowhere."

I was not in a cheerful mood, though. To cheer me up, my friend invited me for ice cream and told me the following story.

The year was 1890. In a small town in eastern Poland, there was a woman whose husband left the house without saying goodbye and did not return for two weeks. The woman was worried and went to ask the priest for guidance. The sexton stopped her at the entrance, and asked why she wanted to see the priest. She explained to him the problem and he let her in.

The priest seeing the woman from afar lowered his eyes to the floor. He did not want to see the woman, fearing that he might get sinful thoughts. The woman told him her story and asked him if her husband would come back.

"Sit here.," said the priest. "Let me consult the Bible and the holy books and I will give you an answer".

After half an hour the priest came back and said to the woman, "Go home and do not worry. Your husband will come back."

The woman was pleased. As she went towards the gate, the sexton asked her, "What did the priest say?" "He said not to worry, my husband will come back."

The sexton looked at her and said, "I am telling you, he will not come back."

The woman was a little confused, but decided that a priest who checked the Bible and the holy books surely knew what he was talking about, and was trustworthier than a sexton.

Four weeks went by and the husband did not come back. The woman decided to go to the priest again. This time the sexton knew already the story and let her in right away.

"My husband did not come back. What shall I do?" said the woman to the priest.

"Stay here a few minutes. Let me consult the Bible and the holy books, and I will give you an answer."

After a few minutes the priest came back and said, "Don't you worry; your husband will come back."

The woman was cheered up. At the gate the sexton asked her again, "What did the priest say this time?"

"Not to worry. My husband will come back."

"And I am telling you, he will not come back."

The woman was upset. She ran back to the priest and told him what the sexton said to her both last time and this time.

The priest became enraged. He asked the sexton, "How dare you to contradict me after I have consulted the Bible and the holy books?"

"Reverend Father," answered the sexton. "You looked up the holy books, so you told her that her husband would come back, but I looked at the woman!"

When my friend finished the story, I felt as if somebody had turned on a light bulb in my head. The sexton was right! To know whether her husband would come back you have to look at the woman not at the holy books! Moreover, to know how often to maintain the barges you have to look at the barges not at the holy book written by an expert!

I thought that I knew what to do. It was the way Joe referred to the consultant's report as "our bible" and "our holy book" that connected the barges to the sexton's story. Sometimes you find great wisdom in simple folk tales. This taught me to listen attentively to stories and try to learn from them.

The next day I spent eight hours watching the barges. Some were in good condition; some were rusty. Some were one or two months after maintenance; some were more than a year.

As I was watching the barges, I got a simple but illuminating idea. It occurred to me that if we could catch the barge just before the last coat of paint was gone there should be no need for chipping. The most expensive and time-consuming element would be eliminated! Of course, if there was no chipping there would be no holes and no need to weld or grind the patches. Wow! These would be real savings!

The next morning I explained the idea to Joe. I asked to make an experiment and to assign to it three barges. These barges would be pulled from the water every week until only the last coat of paint was left. I wanted to see the progress of deterioration for myself and to see whether anything could be done to reduce the yearly maintenance cost.

To make the experiment meaningful, I asked that each of the three coats of paint be of a different color. This would allow me to see when each coat began to wear out and the next coat showed through. There was a resistance to my suggestion. The inventory manager claimed that storing three different colors of paint would increase the inventory, which he was trying to lower as much as possible. I had to go to the vice president to get approval.

I diligently observed what happened to the barges over time, and kept records of what I saw. The life of the coats of paint depended on what the barge was used for. There were special barges assigned to handling chemicals. The paint on these barges wore out sooner.

Next, we experimented with four coats of paint instead of three. The results were amazing. We designed a new method of maintaining barges. Instead of doing it once a year and putting on three coats, we did it every 126 days and put on four coats. The summary of the new method is given below. Even though we calculated that the maintenance would be least expensive if done every 126 days for the sake of simplicity of the comparison, we decided that the new maintenance would be done three times a year. If you compared the new method with the old, you would find that it took fewer man-days to do the maintenance three times a year than it took to do it once a year. Ironically, the manager claimed that he could not do the maintenance even once a year, because he was shorthanded. In the end though, he needed only 18% of man-days to do the maintenance three times a year rather than once a year! (See comparison of the two methods on the following pages).

This, however, was only a small part of the savings. Much greater savings were achieved because of a much longer barge life.

Under the old system, the barge had to be replaced quite often because of the holes caused by chipping and the welding of patches to cover the holes. Eventually the barge was so weakened that it had to be replaced.

Under the new system, a barge could theoretically be used forever, because there was no chipping and no patching. In reality, the barge would have to be replaced but after a much longer period of service then before. I did not stay there long enough to find out what the real savings were.

My friend was right. The idea of how to solve the barge problem came to me unexpectedly while eating ice cream in an ice cream parlor and listening to my friend's story about the sexton. Since then, I applied the sexton's principal of looking at the problem, rather than at the clouds that obscure it. Looking at the issue, not at holy books, reports of experts, or at what other people say. I did so with many projects. It works like a charm.

This story reminds me of what I recently read in William H. Swanson's booklet, "Never be afraid to try something new. Remember, an amateur built an ark that survived a flood while a large group of professionals built the Titanic!

Barge Maintenance - old Method
(1 time per year)

Task	Man days/year
Out of water & back	1
Shaving	1
Chipping	86
Welding & Grinding	11
Painting (3 coats)	3
Total	**102**

Barge Maintenance – New Method
(3 times per year)

Task	Man days/time	Man days/yr
Out of water & back	1	3
Shaving	1	3
Chipping	0	0
Welding	0	0
Painting (4 coats)	4	12
Total	**6**	**18**

I learned that there is no substitute for looking at a problem with your own eyes. Sometimes people will tell you that they have already tried what you have suggested and it did not work. Do not get discouraged. Try it again. Maybe they overlooked something. Maybe you will implement the idea differently and this time it will work. Maybe you will look at the problem from a different perspective, or get more cooperation from others who in the past sabotaged the solution. The main thing is to look at the problem yourself and not through somebody else's eyes. What I learned from the sexton was truly invaluable.

The story did not end here though. What bothered me now was why would a reputable consultant think of doing the maintenance once a year? Why not every nine months or fifteen months? After all the man was not a dummy and had a good reputation. There must have been a good reason why he has recommended maintaining the barges once a year.

I asked people who should know. I tried to find all kinds of reasons but nothing made sense. Then one night it occurred to me what must be the reason: The man recommended maintaining the barges once a year because the earth goes around the sun once a year! If the earth were to go around the sun in eleven month then this would have been a calendar year, and the consultant would still have recommended doing the maintenance once a year, only this time it would have been an eleven-month year! You might think this is crazy. After all, there is no connection whatsoever between maintenance of barges and the time it takes the earth to revolve around the sun. You are right – it is crazy.

While the maintenance of barges has nothing to do with the cycles of celestial bodies, it occurred to me, after a little research, that this consultant is in good company. We do many things based on a calendar year, namely on the time it takes the earth to go around the sun, even though there is no connection between the two issues. For example, we close the books, calculate the profits and pay income tax once a year. In many businesses, this makes no sense. Once in three or five years would give a much better indication of their sales and profits. We make a state budget once a year and politicians have to fight it every twelve months. Why not every twenty or thirty months? I read that a finance minister in Israel suggested that they approve state budgets every two years to reduce the arguing in parliament. Many people do their yearly housecleaning every spring, once every twelve months, not when the house gets dirty.

All annual and semiannual maintenance, oiling of machines and appliances is based not on the needs of the machine but on celestial cycles. It is unfair to single out the consultant of barges and fault him for something that we all do, because the calendar year is an easy schedule to remember.

It then occurred to me that we do many more things without applying the sexton's principle, without looking at the problem. At that time, I had bought a car. The manufacturer recommended it be tuned up every 10,000 miles. I asked myself why every 10,000 miles? I wanted to see how long would the car go without a tune-up. It went 33,251 miles before the car started firing unevenly because of dirty spark plugs, and before it began to show difficulties in starting.

I asked myself why did the manufacturer specify 10,000 miles. It certainly was not based on the needs of the engine. I searched high and low and found only one plausible reason: Because we have ten fingers! This caused the shepherds of old to count the sheep on their fingers and stop every ten. So they had one time ten, two times ten and so on until ten times ten, or a hundred. This, in turn, induced people to develop the decimal system, which is based on the number ten! If we had eight or twelve fingers, our system would probably not be decimal and 10,000 miles would not have been a round number. The manufacturer would have then specified a different round number of miles consistent with eight fingers and the resulting numbering system in use.

When I gave this explanation in one of my management briefings, an attendee suggested that another reason could be greed. The manufacturers may want the motorists to do maintenance more often than needed, in order to sell more spare parts and to let their dealers make more money. This may be true, but this also has nothing to do with the engine's performance. This is another reason to apply the sexton's principle, and to look at the condition of the engine, which is the issue at hand, rather than at other external factors.

Please note that now carmakers have improved the spark plugs and recommend tuning up your engine every 100,000 miles, which is also based on us having ten fingers! I would be surprised if the engine knew that we have ten fingers and, therefore, a decimal system, and that because of that it should start skipping and sputtering at a round number of 100,000 miles!

The longer I live, the more I appreciate the sexton's principle. We do many things without looking at the issues but rather at the clouds that obscure them. These clouds could be "holy books" like manuals, or our ego, or wishful thinking. This is true of politicians, businessmen and simple folks dealing with their spouses and children. This explains why Chamberlain made peace with Hitler. It was wishful thinking, not looking at the issues. This is also the reason why so many businesses close after being open for only one or two years, and why only 5% of new businesses survive after five years. All these entrepreneurs did not look at the real issues but at the clouds that obscured them.

Next time you pray, maybe you should consider also saying a short prayer for our sexton. He has certainly earned it.

The Sexton's Principle

Chapter 11

Changing the President's Image

> Everyone thinks of changing the world, but no one thinks of changing himself.
>
> — *Leo Tolstoy*

The way people perceive us has a great impact on how they relate to us. However people interpret our behavior based on their beliefs, expectations and preconceptions. This is why a person's image depends only in part on what he says and does. Thus, you may find that even though a community leader does a decent job and does his best to project a good image, some community members will disdain him anyway.

Managers face the same problem. No matter how hard they try, some employees will think that they are not fair, or are not doing their job well.

I faced this problem on a grand scale when I took on a project in California. The company, Valor Computerized Systems, was a wholly owned subsidiary of an overseas software house and was marketing proprietary software in the United States and Canada. The president started as the company's only salesman, but by now the company had grown to thirty-five employees including twelve salesmen and ten engineers.

Chuck Feingold, the president, was an open-minded man. He booked my briefing on "Managing to Encourage Change." After the briefing, he asked me to do a unique project. He wanted me to help him find out what, if anything, he was doing wrong and how he could correct it. Truthfully, I was somewhat taken aback, much impressed with the maturity and humility of someone who would ask for such a project.

I began the project by interviewing twenty key managers and employees. Together we found sixteen issues that the majority believed could be improved. However, nearly all of the participants agreed on one important issue. After listening and analyzing what I had heard, I classified it as a problem of perception.

"We do not have a president," said the director of engineering.

"What do you mean?" I asked. "Isn't Chuck your president?"

"Well he is in name. Actually though, Chuck is out of the office most of the time, selling software. He's a super salesman, and he really likes selling. He was selling when he started the company, and he is still selling now."

I heard a similar story from seventeen people. From what I could see, the company was run reasonably well. However, the managers and employees perceived Chuck as a salesman rather than as a president. I realized that the only way to resolve this issue was by changing their perception. I decided to correct this problem, even though it was not part of my assignment in any formal way.

"Maybe you're right." I said to Greg, the director of engineering. "I'm new here and know nothing about the company. What value does the company create to justify its existence? What does it produce?"

"Actually, the company doesn't produce anything. It distributes what the software house produces."

"You mean to say that all this company does is market and sell what the software house produces?"

"Pretty much so", said Greg.

"If a company were to produce machinery, would you say that in addition to being a good manager, a president should also be a good engineer, and be able to intelligently discuss design issues with the engineering department and key customers?"

"I suppose so," said Greg.

"If you had to recruit a president for Ford Motor Company what kind of skills and education would you want the candidates to have, in addition to being a good manager of large companies?"

"I think it would help if the man were an experienced automotive engineer so that he could communicate with his engineers on the production floor and with R&D."

"Using the same reasoning, what qualifications should a president of a large accounting firm have?"

Greg thought for a minute and suggested that the president should have good accounting skills, to be able to help his staff with difficult problems, and personally provide advice to larger clients.

"In line with your reasoning, what skills should have a president of a company, that is engaged solely in selling? Wouldn't you say that he should be a good salesman, so that he can close the most important sales and also give support to his sales-people when they require it?"

"I never thought about it that way," answered Greg.

"That's okay. Think it over; it makes sense. In fact you were the one who suggested it."

Greg thought about it for a while and in the end agreed. Now I had a method that worked for one man. Of course, there was no guarantee that it would work on the remaining sixteen, but I was willing to try.

Tom, the customer service manager, agreed in principal with Greg but still claimed that Chuck devoted to much time to sales and too little to managing. However, when pressed for examples of what was neglected due to this imbalance, he could not produce even one example. Finally, he agreed that Chuck was not a bad president, but that in his opinion he should spend less time in sales. I explained to him that as a president, Chuck had to set his priorities according to the needs of the company as he saw them. I also said, that being a super salesman, it was only natural that he would stress sales more than other aspects of his job.

I met one on one with other key employees of the company. Some of them had reservations but in the end every one of them came to the conclusion that Chuck was a good president.

After the project was completed, Chuck told me that he could see a difference in how managers and employees related to him. He said, "This was simply an issue of difference in perception. I believe that now their perceptions are closer to my own."

It appears that Chuck was not satisfied just with the change of perception of his employees. He listened to what they said and tried to learn from it as evident from the letter below.

Dear Henry,

I have no problem with the use of real names in your book regarding Valor. Our lesson can be others' lesson.

What is interesting is that my take home (amongst other things) from the work we did with you was to relate more to each part of the organization equally. Working to understand and partake much more in the engineering side of Valor. Knowing that I would not lose the sales centric part of my day-to-day work, I started focusing on the engineering and even the administration side of the company. Ultimately this became a key factor in growing the company to the next level as a "president" and not as a "salesman".

Best regards,
        Chuck

Chapter 12

Information Systems Pitfalls

> If you put tomfoolery into a computer, nothing comes out of it but tomfoolery. But this tomfoolery, having passed through a very expensive machine, is somehow ennobled and no one dares criticize it.
> — *Pierre Gallois*

Information systems can save you a lot of money and aggravation. Today it is almost impossible to think of running a business without computers. However there are some pitfalls that management should be aware of and prepared for.

I recall that some time ago when I was working on an assignment in Canada, I went to the only supermarket in town to buy a carton of milk. I brought the milk to the register and the clerk told me that he could not sell me the milk because the computers were down. I could hardly believe my ears. They needed a computer to sell me a pint of milk! The supermarket did not function for six hours. The lines of disappointed customers were growing, and I overheard one customer saying with bitter humour that in the future he would bring a loaf of bread with him when going to the supermarket bakery, to avoid starving from hunger before being served. How did they do it twenty years ago when there were no computers in supermarkets? Obviously the managers of this supermarket did not plan for contingencies.

Another problem is the question of responsibility. I first encountered this problem in inventory control. When the inventory system of a client of mine was computerized, many employees felt relieved from the heavy responsibility of making decisions of what, when and how much to order, because "The computer will do it." I recall a case of a company president who reprimanded his purchasing agent for buying too few items of a stock-keeping unit (SKU), which resulted in a shutdown of a production line. The purchasing agent answered: "What do you want from me? I just followed the instructions given to me by the computer."

It is important to stress that a computer is only a tool. The responsibility rests with the user of the tool, in this case with the purchasing agent. Think of it as a case of delegation. When you delegate a task to a computer it is like delegating a task to a low-level employee. You must review what the employee has done and you are responsible for the consequences.

Another case, which happened to one of my clients, illustrates the dangers of complacency resulting from excessive reliance on information systems in making decisions. This company was a large tire distributor. Most tires distributed by this company were expensive large tires for airplanes often selling for more than $1000 each. The company had a sophisticated inventory control system with moving averages, exponential smoothing and many other bells and whistles. The system tracked the demand for every SKU each month and was programmed to forecast the demand for every SKU in the months ahead, based on past data. When the inventory level of a given tire hit the order point, the order was automatically printed and could be sent to the vendor by modem.

Due to personnel turnover, a new purchasing agent was hired in July, in the section that handled the 100z tires. He felt a little insecure in the new job, but his supervisor, the sales manager, who joined the company only two months earlier, told him not to worry, because the computer system was sophisticated and supposedly very reliable, and would tell him what, when, and how much to order.

The computer, after calculating the moving average and after exponential smoothing, projected the new demand for the 100z tire for the month of September, and recommended ordering 500 tires, which were delivered at the end of August.

When I was called to help the company with their inventory problems in December, the sales manager told me that something must be wrong with the forecasting system, because a number of items did not sell as projected. I asked him to name the worst case and he mentioned the 100z tires: "Five hundred tires arrived in August and only three were sold by mid December."

My job was not easy. The new purchasing agent knew nothing about the history of the tire, and his supervisor, who had been with the company only two months longer, was not much help either. I tried to find someone who worked with the 100z tire a year before. Finally, I was told that Nancy, who had been the assistant buyer in the tire section, and whose job had been eliminated, still worked for the company. She had been moved to the accounting department.

I invited Nancy for lunch and over a hot bowl of soup and a generous sandwich she explained, that there was really nothing special she could tell me about the 100z tire. Well, I said to myself, there may after all be such a thing as a free lunch – Nancy just got one. I continued probing, "How were sales of the 100z tire last year? " I asked.

"Very slow", answered Nancy.

After a little prodding Nancy recalled that at beginning of September a year ago, there were about seven hundred 100z tires in stock at a cost of $800 each, and they were selling at a rate of one or two a month. The reason was that another company designed a similar tire. This new tire was better than the 100z tire and was less expensive.

The most important piece of the puzzle I extracted from Nancy just before the waiter handed me the check. When I asked her what happened with the remaining 100z tires, Nancy told me that in order to get rid of the slow moving 100z tires, the previous sales manager decided to cut the price by 50% and sell them at a loss. By the end of September, all 100z tires were sold, not even one was left in the warehouse.

Aha! I said to myself. This is the key to the riddle! Since seven hundred tires were sold in September last year, the computer duly registered that September is a hot month for selling 100z tires, and followed the sequence of steps to ensure ample supply of 100z tires for September of this year. Needless to say, the company was stuck with 500 tires at $800 each, and had to repeat the half price sale to get rid of the $400,000 inventory of obsolete merchandise and lost $200,000 in the process.

As you can see from this case study, you cannot let your guards down and rely completely on what the computer tells you. The computer is an excellent working tool and can make your job much easier but it needs someone with brains to use it, to ensure the validity of inputs and outputs and make the final decisions.

Well, I said to myself, there is no such thing as free lunch after all. Nancy did not get one either – she earned it.

Chapter 13

The Power of Encouragement

The worst mistake a boss can make is not to say, "Well done."
— *John Ashcroft*

Josh was twelve years old. His 5th grade teacher thought highly of him. He was always a good student – his grades and homework were always excellent.

At the beginning of the sixth grade however, there was a marked change in Josh's performance. He often forgot to do his homework and when he did it the quality was poor. His appearance had also changed. He often came to school unkempt, his shirt soiled, his shoes dirty, his notebooks stained. Sometimes he did not come to school at all. The teacher called his parents and left numerous messages, none of which were answered.

The youth club counselor, Tim, wondered why Josh had stopped coming to activities. In the past, Josh had been a regular attendee and Tim thought that they were on good terms, especially since the time Tim saved Josh from two teenagers who had attacked him in the street, in order to steal his money.

One afternoon Tim got a call from the police. They asked him if he could come to the police station. It was about Josh, and it was urgent.

When Tim arrived at the station, the officer in charge told him that Josh was part of a gang that had beaten up three boys and had stolen their bicycles. Josh could be indicted in juvenile court and sent to a correction facility, unless an adult would vouch for his future behavior. The police called Josh's home, but there was no answer. That was when Josh gave Tim's name.

Tim asked to speak with Josh in private. When Josh was brought to Tim he was crying. He told Tim that his father had died four months ago. His mother had taken a job as a waitress and was busy all day long. In the evening, she was tired and impatient. She would scream at Josh and his seven-year-old brother at the slightest infraction. Josh was now responsible for preparing breakfast for himself and his brother and sending him to school. Josh joined the gang, which had become his new home. There he found new friends, but now they were all in custody and Josh did not know whom to turn to.

Tim explained to Josh the severity of the situation. He told him that he believed in him, because he knew him well. He understood that the gang was bad influence on him, and knew that if it were up to Josh, he would never steal or beat-up innocent boys. Yes, if Josh agreed to give-up being in the gang and made a serious commitment to becoming a good student and doing what was required of him, Tim was willing to personally vouch for him. Tim also explained to Josh that the alternative was much worse.

Josh started sobbing loudly. Tim embraced him and calmed him down.

"So what is your decision?" asked Tim.

Josh did not answer. He started sobbing again. When Tim embraced him again Josh hugged him back and said: "Get me out of here, and I will do anything you ask me to."

Tim signed the necessary papers and they went to the youth club. The boys in the club did not know what had happened and started playing with Josh as they had in the old days. Some asked why he had been away for two months, but Tim explained that he had been busy helping his mother and taking care of his younger brother.

Tim checked on Josh daily, helped him with homework as needed and was in touch with his teachers on a regular basis. He told Josh how proud he was of his progress. Josh went on to become an excellent student. After finishing high school, he went to college and graduate school and received a degree in public administration.

Upon graduation, Josh started working for the municipality, and in a short time became director of youth activities. In this capacity, he helped Tim save many boys and girls who had fallen on hard times. He said to Tim, "When I needed help you were there for me. You believed in me and encouraged me. Were it not for your encouragement and help I would have probably stayed with the gang and be now dead or imprisoned for life. Now I want to do what I can to help others stay out of trouble." Tim and Josh became friends for life.

We can learn from this story that encouragement can change a man's performance, and even change his life. Encouragement is especially helpful when one feels that he is not equal to the task he is facing. You often see managers or supervisors who are insecure, and are afraid to make decisions because they are afraid to fail and therefore do not act. They forget that not acting is also a decision, and can itself lead to failure. In such cases encouragement can be very helpful.

Even very capable executives are not immune to underestimating and doubting themselves. Many of us feel insecure when facing important decisions in personal life or in business. This is the time when we need encouragement, moral support and someone to talk to. This is a situation where a trustworthy consultant can be invaluable.

Some years ago I worked with a very capable marketing manager of a west coast company. Given the opportunity the man could become a successful president of a company. When the incumbent president died, the board of directors decided to look for a seasoned executive outside the company to fill the vacancy. I suggested to Dan, the marketing manager, to approach the board of directors and ask to be considered as a candidate for the vacant position. He answered: "The board of directors will never choose me. I never managed more than five salesmen."

I explained to him that he had other advantages to compensate for lack of managerial experience. In the past he introduced many new products. Some of them became best sellers and increased significantly company sales. He had excellent relations with company customers and was liked by company managers, employees and members of the board of directors. I also mentioned that many presidents of large companies started in sales and marketing. However, Dan was not persuaded.

"Why would they risk losing a relatively good marketing manager to gain a poor president? In the end they may lay me off and I will have no job at all." he said.

I could sense that he was reluctant to go to the board of directors to avoid the possibility of rejection. Dan was an unassuming man, and despite his ability was not sure that he could be a good president. I saw the man's potential and I believed in him. I told him so.

Dan was still afraid that the board of directors would say that he lacked the experience required for the job. I told him,

"How do you know what they will say? If they feel you do not have the necessary experience, let them tell you so. Besides, if you go to them they may say 'yes' or they may say 'no'. However, if you do not go at all, you have already said 'no' to yourself even before you have tried. Why would you want do this to yourself? I have confidence in you. I am still the company's consultant and I will help you succeed."

To alleviate the doubts of the board of directors, I suggested that he offer them to appoint him as president for an interim period of one year. If he succeeded, the board would stop looking for a suitable candidate. Otherwise, he would go back to his position as the marketing manager of the company and help the new president, whom they would appoint. This would be an acceptable, no risk, "win - win" solution for both the board of directors and the marketing director.

This gave him the encouragement he needed. He went to the board of directors and two weeks later got the job. He became an excellent president. He increased yearly sales of the company from eighty million dollars a year to over four hundred million dollars in less than seven years.

Encouragement is needed not only in case of promotion as we saw above but sometimes also in case of demotion as illustrated in the following example.

An honest, capable and well-liked project engineer who had been with the company for ten years was promoted to a position of engineering manager of an eight hundred million dollar company, supervising more than fifty engineers. After two years, it became obvious that he was not suitable for the job. He was an excellent project engineer when supervising five or six engineers but a poor manager of the large department. The president of the company who promoted him and was himself an engineer tried to help him. However, nothing seemed to work. Management decided to replace him as soon as a suitable candidate was found. I thought that terminating the man would be a loss to the company because he knew a lot about the business and was an exceptional engineer.

When I met the man, he looked tired and nervous. He had red rings around the eyes. I asked him how things were going and whether he was happy in his position. He was quite open and told me that the president was not happy with his performance and for good reasons. This made him tense. He could not sleep at night. He knew that he had disappointed the man who promoted him. He was at his wits' end and did not know what to do.

The problem that he faced could be reduced to a simple question: was it better to be an unhappy engineering manager or a happy engineer. I asked him, "How much is being happy worth to you? Would you agree to take a job that makes you unhappy if they doubled your pay?"

He replied, "I would rather make less and be happy."

I asked him if he would return to his old job even if that meant a 25% cut in his salary. I pointed out to him that money was not of primary importance at this stage of his life. He was over fifty years old and his children were married. He needed to support only himself and his wife, and probably had accumulated some wealth from savings and stock options that were doing quite well recently. He agreed with me and added, "When I leave this world, I can't take it with me anyway."

The remaining question was his ego. Would pride and vanity prevent him from making the right decision? Would he rather leave the company than suffer, what others might consider loss of face? He answered all these questions with maturity. He had been with the company a long time and would like to stay. He realized that at his age it would not be easy to find another suitable job.

One problem remained though. He was afraid that the company would not let him stay as an engineer. Some companies prefer to terminate employees rather then demote them, because they believe that demotion is bad for morale. I tried to reassure him, but I sensed that he lacked confidence.

We developed together a strategy to overcome this problem as follows. He would approach his boss and tell him that he was unhappy being manager of engineering. He knew that he lacked the skills needed to manage many people and he always had the feeling that he was holding the company back. He thought that he could contribute much more to the company's growth as a project engineer and could be of great help to the new engineering manager. If the company would let him do it, he would be a happy man again.

We did some role-playing. First, he was the boss and I was the employee. Then we reversed the roles. Next day he called me and told me that the meeting with the president had been successful.

From above examples, we can learn two important lessons. Firstly, it is important to encourage people to do the right things. Sometimes the right thing is to be demoted. Secondly, we should never get discouraged trying to guess what other people think.

Chapter 14

Penny-wise, Dollar-foolish

> The easiest thing of all is to deceive one's self; for what a man wishes he generally believes to be true.
>
> – *Demosthenes*

One day I got a call from the president of a stock brokerage. The company dealt mainly in bonds. Stocks were sold only as an accommodation to clients. The president complained that in the last few months sales had decreased. He wanted me to review the operation and suggest changes to improve it.

When I came to visit the president for the first time, he proudly showed me the elegant, newly refurbished conference room where he received his most important clients. The large open floor where the brokers sat at their desks and made calls to clients also looked brand new. "We purchased a new wall-to-wall carpet for almost $100,000 few months ago, because the old one was stained. I was embarrassed when visitors saw the dirty surroundings. I thought that a new carpet was a good investment that would impress existing and potential clients. We have also purchased a number of new desks to replace the old ones. As you see I am not afraid to make changes even if this means spending hard cash."

I spent a few days getting acquainted with people and observing the operation. It soon became obvious that the only way a broker could get an order was by talking to the client on the phone.

Having observed the operation, I concluded that the brokers spent only a fraction of their time on the phone, perhaps as little as 20%. However, I knew that if I told them how little time they spent on the phone they would not believe me or, even worse, they might become insulted and be afraid that I might tell the president how poorly they performed.

Since I did not want to offend the brokers and managers, I employed my interactive consulting method, and suggested that the managers themselves determine the percentage of time spent on the phone.

Their answer was, "We do not have time to do it. Besides, we do not know how to do time studies."

I answered, "Do not worry. I will show you a simple method. You will learn it in fifteen minutes. It will take each of you about three minutes a day for a period of four weeks.

I showed the mangers how to determine the distribution of time by taking readings at random intervals and posting tally strokes in the appropriate row on a card as described in the chapter entitled "A Matter of Faith." They learned how to determine how much time was spent on the phone, how much on record keeping, talking, walking, being absent from the desk, and so on. The managers took readings and I took readings too, to make sure that the results were objective.

After a few days, I made friends with some brokers and broker trainees. Many of them told me that they did not like the new carpet

"Why?" I asked.

They explained to me that before the new carpet was installed everyone could go down to the cafeteria, which was in the basement, buy what he wanted and bring it upstairs to his desk where he could eat and drink at his leisure, doing some work and answering telephone calls from clients.

" But what has this got to do with the new wall to wall carpet?" I asked.

"Everything" was the answer. "You see, the old carpet was here for ten years or more. In time, it became stained from food and spilled drinks. They only vacuumed the carpet but never washed out the stains, which became set over time and could not be removed. The new carpet was quite expensive. The president wanted to keep it clean to impress new clients. He was afraid that it would get stained, so he told us to eat and drink only downstairs in the cafeteria".

That was how I got my education. I was asked not to mention to the president what they told me, because this was his "hot button". Sparkling clean offices were his obsession. He thought that the new carpet would improve business.

Following the Sexton's principle I decided to see first hand what happens in the cafeteria. At ten o'clock in the morning I went downstairs and bought a cup of coffee. There were a few tables and chairs for customers. I found an empty chair at a table occupied by two old-time brokers and a broker trainee. The conversation centered on recent television movies and later on sports. After twenty minutes, the trainee got up and explained that he has to rush back upstairs because he had to finish his quota of successful calls. The old timers were in no hurry. One of them started reading the sports section of the newspaper. The other went to buy more coffee and another croissant. At ten forty, both brokers returned upstairs. I followed one of them to find out what happened in his absence. His secretary told him that there were three calls, two from clients and one from his wife. He decided to call the clients first. One client was in a rush to leave for Chicago and promised to call again next week. The other client had called thirty minutes before and wanted to buy a stock, but decided not to, because the price had gone up by fifty-two cents by the time the broker returned his call.

The old timers were generally more relaxed and less anxious to call customers than the trainees. They knew that their customer base was large enough to give them a substantial income and increasing their take-home check was not their first priority.

I continued my observations at lunchtime. The cafeteria started filling up at eleven thirty. At twelve o'clock, it was nearly full. The old timers took a longer lunch break. A few of them stretched it to one and quarter hours. Most of them were out after about one hour. The trainees took a much shorter break, usually between thirty and forty minutes.

At three o'clock, the same thing happened, as at ten o'clock, though the crowd was smaller. The cafeteria was never empty during the day. There always were seven or eight brokers sitting there talking, reading and discussing various topics. It was a place to hang out, where you could always find some company to chat about interesting things.

I estimated that on the average one-hour and a quarter was wasted on walking down and returning to work, talking, reading and other non-productive activities, not including the official thirty minutes for lunch and fifteen minutes each for morning and afternoon breaks. Most brokers and trainees worked more than the regular seven hours from nine to five. They came earlier and stayed longer, averaging about eight work-hours a day. Thus, the wasted time amounted to one and a quarter hour out of eight hours or about 15.6%.

In the meantime, the managers finished their time distribution survey and concluded, that about 21% of time was spent on the phone. The managers were surprised and disappointed that the percentage was so low. Despite that no one complained that the results were wrong. How could they complain? They were the ones who made the survey.

Now I had all the information I needed to discuss the issues with the president. He agreed with me that talking with clients on the phone was a prerequisite to getting an order. It was the most productive element leading to company profits. He was surprised that only twenty one percent of time was spent on the telephone. He was even more surprised when I showed him that the time wasted in the cafeteria was almost three quarters of the time spent on the telephone (15.6% / 21% = 0.74). Suddenly, it occurred to him, that if we could use this wasted time making calls to clients, the profit of the company could increase by nearly seventy five percent!

I agreed with him only partially. First, it was unlikely that all of the wasted time would be used to make or answer calls. Secondly, even if this were possible, the volume of orders might not increase in proportion to the number of calls made, because of the law of diminishing returns.

I explained to the president that the best way to save the wasted time would be to have a coffee man bring the food and drinks to the broker's table, and free the brokers from the need to leave their desks. We calculated that even if the profits increased only by ten percent, there would be enough money to distribute all the food and drinks to every one on the floor free of charge, clean the carpet thoroughly every month, replace it when needed and still increase company profits by million dollars.

The president reluctantly agreed to allow eating on the floor. He objected, however, to distribution of food free of charge. At the end, though, he compromised and agreed to distribute free drinks and cakes at ten AM and three PM. The employees still had to pay for lunch.

I have encountered many examples of managers bent on small savings that caused bigger losses in the process. I know a company president who himself checks daily if all lights are out after hours to save electricity. He could save much more if he delegated the checking of lights to a low-level employee and spent his time paying attention to larger expenses. Later I was told that his mother used to tell him to turn off the unused lights when he was a boy and he was still doing it today. Similarly, some people are upset when overcharged fifty cents for orange juice at the supermarket but are not nearly as disturbed when they lose ten thousand dollars on a stock. Sometimes small losses disturb us more than big ones. It is an emotional reaction not related to the magnitude of the loss. If you look around your workplace, you will surely find examples where your company is saving pennies and losing dollars.

Chapter 15

Teaching Old Dogs New Tricks

> There are only two ways to live your life: One is as though nothing is a miracle. The other is as if everything is. I believe in the latter.
> – *Albert Einstein*

A client of mine advised his friend to book my management briefing on "Managing to Encourage Change." When I walked through his friend's plant, I noticed that the company needed a great deal of help and a great deal of change. The management briefing was well attended and the participants were active and asked good questions.

After the briefing the president came to me and said, "Everything looks different to me now. I feel like I am wearing glasses of a different color." He invited me for a cup of tea in his office, and asked me where I worked and what I had accomplished there. Then he asked me what I thought of his plant and his managers, who participated in the briefing. He was pleased with my answers. He liked my interactive consulting method, and I was sure that we would soon sign an agreement. I told him what to expect in terms of savings and increased profits. I thought that he agreed with me. Then suddenly he said that even though he thought highly of me and was impressed with my ability, he believed that it had been decreed in heaven how much he would earn this year, and that I could not change this, no matter what I did.

I was caught by surprise. This was an objection I had never encountered before, and did not know how to overcome. It took me a few seconds to regain my composure. I recalled that one of my mentors, taught me never to argue with people about their religious beliefs, because it would not help, and could create animosity. I realized that I should work within his frame of reasoning rather then try to change it. I had to understand what would make sense to him from his point of view and work accordingly. On the other hand, I did not want to say something that I did not believe in. I had to find an approach that I could live with and that would make sense to the prospective client.

"You are absolutely right." I said. "I agree with you one hundred percent that I cannot change what has been decreed in heaven; I am only the messenger."

"What do you mean by that?" asked the president.

To make my point I told him the story about the righteous priest who had a church in a small town. He was always helping the poor, the widows and the orphans. Members of his congregation liked him, and he was ready to give his life, if needed, to serve his flock.

One day, heavy rains caused a flood. The level of water in the river was higher than anyone could remember. Everybody was trying to save himself. Many people left their homes, and the mayor of the town urged the priest to leave the church, but to no avail. His response was: "I was always faithful to my people and my church. I am not going to abandon them now, in their hour of need. I am confident that God will not let me die."

The flood got worse. The level of water was getting higher every minute. The mayor sent a boat to save the priest. The priest explained that he could not leave now, when his church was in danger. In the meantime, the water level kept rising. The mayor sent another boat and a member of the town council to persuade the priest. However, the priest repeated that he could not leave, that he always lived a pure life and that he was confident that somehow he would be saved.

An hour later, the water filled the church and the priest climbed on the top of the steeple. The mayor sent his private helicopter to save the priest, but the priest refused. He kept repeating, "I have faith in heaven and I am confident that I will be saved."

Two hours later, they found his body floating in the river. When the priest arrived at the pearly gates he complained to the angel who received him, "I always led a pure life, did good deeds and was faithful to my church and my flock. Why was I abandoned in my hour of need?"

A deep voice in heaven answered, "Did I not send two boats and a helicopter to save you?"

The president got the message. Within a few minutes, we signed a contract. However, this was not the end of the story. The company was growing fast. In a few years, sales had increased from twenty million dollars to a hundred and twenty million dollars.

The general manager was a capable but very conservative religious man about sixty-five years old. He liked to micro-manage the operation. For him delegation was out of the question, because he did not rely on anybody else. The president relied on him to run the company but was concerned because as the company grew, there was much more to do and the present general manager could not do it all. He had hired some low-level help, but the president thought that this was not enough. The president's other concern was what would happen in the future. The general manager did not hire any suitable successor, and made sure that he was indispensable. "What would we do if Michael, the general manager, got sick or decided to retire?" the president asked me.

The president wanted me to help design an organization that would address the present needs of the company and would provide for future expansion and management succession. He warned me that the job would not be easy because Michael was resisting change and refused to work with consultants.

My first meeting with Michael was less than friendly. He told me that the president hired in the past consultants to help him. The last one was hired two years ago but he, Michael, got rid of him because he had no use for consultants, especially if they were not fast with figures or had difficulties reading P&L statements and balance sheets.

"Great" I said, "You did the right thing, I do not believe in consultants either."

Michael was caught by surprise. He said, "Whom are you kidding? Aren't you a consultant?"

"No, I am not." I answered, "I do not do what consultants do. I do not write reports, I make no recommendations and I do not tell people what to do. Since I do not do these three things how can I be a consultant?"

"Then what do you do. How do you help your clients?"

I explained to Michael my interactive consulting method, and how he would always be in charge of what we designed and how we implemented it. I told him that it was my strong conviction, that the people who would live with the changes had to be involved in their design.

Michael was somewhat skeptical, but was not sure how to respond. We spent the rest of the meeting just becoming acquainted with each other. Michael, knew the Bible inside out, peppered the conversation with Biblical quotations, and towards the end of the meeting, I was somewhat optimistic that we might be able to establish a working relationship.

When we next met, I asked Michael to describe the present organization to me and to describe what changes he would suggest in order to improve it. He thought that the organization did not need any improvement. To prove it he showed me that sales had increased almost six-fold in the last eight years under the present organization.

I still did not give up. I asked him, "Do you think that the same organization is needed to manage effectively a hundred and twenty million dollar company as a twenty million dollar company?"

"I did not give it much thought. Besides, you cannot teach an old dog new tricks."

By now, I understood that the best way to persuade him was to find some supporting examples from the Bible.

"First, you are not a dog. You are a human being." I said. "Secondly, you are not old, at least in comparison to me. Thirdly, I was not talking about new tricks. These tricks are three thousand years old."

"What are you talking about?" asked Michael.

"I am talking about Moses. He tried to manage his huge flock all by himself, until his father in law, Jethro, told him that he must learn to delegate or perish because of the unbearable workload. Maybe you can help me with the exact quote."

Michael corrected me and quoted the exact words from the Bible. I suggested that Michael follow Jethro's advice, which was still valid today. We agreed to meet in a week and discuss the new organization that Michael would design and that his assistant would draw on the computer.

A week later Michael showed me the organizational chart that he designed. It was almost the same as the present organization.

I wanted to give him encouragement, so I decided not criticize his chart. Instead, I said that this was one feasible option. However having only one option was always risky, because it could be the worst option possible. We needed more options so we could pick one that might be better. Moreover, if we had, say, four options we could use the pairing of options method and develop a fifth option better than the original four. I explained to Michael my pairing of options method and he liked it.

We decided to meet next week. This would give Michael time to design three more options. The following Tuesday we discussed the four options. I asked him what he would like to do when the company would increase to two hundred million dollars in sales. He smiled and said that he would like to be the

CEO. I pointed out that he could not be promoted unless someone was trained to take over his duties. He thought that there was no one in the organization capable of doing it.

After a little coaching, Michael decided that a new manager should be hired and trained to become general manager in the future.

When we developed the new organizational structure by the pairing of options method, I suggested that Michael should write a brief report to present the new structure for the president's approval. He did not like the idea. He told me that he had to run the company and had no time to write reports. He added that he was sure that neither Moses nor Jethro wrote reports. I told him that I had the time and would gladly write a draft for him, which he could correct. He could delete what he did not like and add what I missed. His name would appear on the cover, because it was his project.

Next week I brought a draft for his correction and approval. On the front page, I listed him as the author. He objected. He said: "Erase me from your book." quoting Moses from the Bible. He insisted that I wrote the report and, therefore, I was the author.

I thought that it was important for him to sign the report and feel that he was the one who suggested the changes. I explained to him that the project was his, since the ideas in the report were his. In the end, he agreed to sign the report together with me. I made sure to list his name first and my name second.

It is not easy for someone to change his management style in one day. Learning how to delegate is difficult for someone who is suspicious and does not trust anybody. This can only be done gradually over a long period. Just like water dripping on a stone makes no mark after just a day or two, but if the water drips for a few years it will eventually make a dimple in it.

I thought that Michael made a lot of progress in his management thinking. The president told me that this was the first time that Michael realized that delegation could be a good thing. After Michael presented him with the report and returned to the plant, the president said to me: "It is truly a miracle! You managed to teach an old dog new tricks."

Chapter 16

Persistence Pays

> 80% of all sales are made after the fifth call.
> 48% of salesmen give up after the first call
> 25% give up after the second call
> A mere 12% of salesmen make more than five calls
> To this persistent 12% go 80% of all sales
>
> — *The National Retail Dry Goods Association*

I had just finished a project for an overseas client and was returning home. It was a long flight and I was tired of sitting in one place without much movement. The flight attendant took the tray from the table in front of my seat and I readied myself to take a walk in the airplane to stretch my limbs.

As I reached the tail of the airplane, I saw a man walking in place. "Are you exercising to prevent your feet from becoming numb?" I asked. "Yes, it helps. It is important for me, since in my business I fly very often." answered the stranger.

"May I ask what the nature of your business is?" I asked.

"Sure, I am Gary Stone the Chairman and CEO of Stanton Corporation."

"My name is Henry Ekstein. It is my pleasure to meet you. Isn't Stanton the multi-billion dollar manufacturing equipment company?"

"Yes, mostly for heavy manufacturing. And may I ask what business are you in?"

"I help companies grow."

"I have no use for consultants. There is nothing they can do for my company."

"I agree with you one hundred percent. Consultants cannot help you."

"I do not understand what you are saying. Aren't you a consultant?"

"No. I am not. I do not write reports, I do not make recommendations, and I do not tell people what to do. People mistakenly call me a consultant because they do not know what else to call me."

"If you do not do these three things, how do you help companies grow?"

"And if I did these three things, how could I help my clients? You yourself said that consultants cannot do anything for a company."

"You told me what you do not do. But you still did not tell me what you do. How do you help your clients? Do you know the answers to all their problems?"

"I admit that I do not know the answers to their problems, but I know how to ask the right questions. When I ask managers the right questions this opens, broadens and stretches their minds, and they find the right answers. I have developed a theory why and how my approach works. I have been doing it for more than twenty years and I've found it to be very effective."

"Do you have anything you can give me in writing?"

"More than fifty articles, cover stories and letters to the editor have been written about my work; I would be happy to give you a few reprints. By the way, a vice president of ADP, who attended my management briefing on "Managing to Encourage Change", suggested that I not call myself a consultant but a management mind stretcher. In a letter to the editor to Success magazine he wrote, 'Perhaps Oliver Wendell Holmes best expressed my experience with Dr. Ekstein when he said that Man's mind once stretched by a new idea, never regains it's original dimensions.' Do you think that I should call myself 'management mind stretcher'?"

"Yes, I like it. It is much better than 'consultant'."

I said to myself, if two top executives of Fortune 500 companies told me the same thing, I had better listen. This is how I started calling myself a management mind stretcher. A new profession was born.

I gave Gary a few reprints, describing my work and my management briefings. I asked him to call me and let me know if he liked my theories and whether there was anything I could do to help his company. He agreed to get back to me.

Frankly, I was very impressed with Gary. Despite his high position, he appeared to be a humble man who addressed people with respect. He treated me as an equal. When we talked, I had the feeling that I had known him for many years.

Two weeks went by and I did not hear from Gary. I decided to call him and ask whether he had had a chance to read the articles. His secretary told me that he was in China. When I called a week later, I was told he was in Hungary. A few days later, he was somewhere in Asia. When I called next time, he was in a meeting.

I said to myself that perhaps I should stop calling. Maybe he did not like my theories or did not want to do business with me, and his secretary had simply provided excuses in order not to offend me.

The next day I went to a client, a manufacturer who wanted to sell his products to a large home-improvement chain.

My client called the buyer a number of times, and left messages with his secretary, but his calls were never returned.

My client stopped calling the prospect. "I met this buyer once last year. Maybe he does not want to buy from me because he does not like me. Maybe he is happy with his present supplier. Maybe he thinks that I am too small to handle his business. Perhaps he is afraid that I will be unable to provide good service," the client told me. I could sense that he was afraid of rejection. "The deepest principle in human nature is the craving to be appreciated," said philosopher William James. Rejection violates this principle; it is the opposite of appreciation. Hence, the strong fear of rejection we all have.

I asked him, "How can you assume what other men think? Are you a mind reader?"

"No, I am not a mind reader," answered my client.

"Could all this be in your head, because you are afraid of rejection? Is it possible that the man was simply too busy to answer your calls?"

"What do you want me to do?" asked my client.

"I never tell people what to do. The decision should be yours, but let me ask you a question. If you keep calling your prospect he may buy from you or he may not. However, if you do not call him, it is almost certain that he will not buy from you. That being the case what would you rather do?"

"I should probably call him. If he does not want me to call him, let him tell me so."

"I think you reached the right decision." I said.

My client called the prospect again and made an appointment to see him. When I asked him later how the meeting had gone, he told me that the buyer had been happy to see him. He was having terrible service problems with his present supplier, who was so big that he could not deal with the small problems of every single customer. The buyer wanted a smaller reputable supplier, for whom he would be an important customer, and who would give him good service. He liked my client's reputation and was willing to give him a small trial order. A day later, my client booked an order and thus opened a new account.

"How wrong I was." said my client. "If you had not encouraged me to call, I would have lost this account."

"Do not blame yourself. It is human nature to assume the worst to avoid disappointment. Nevertheless, it is sometimes good to remind ourselves, that we cannot guess what other people think; we are not mind readers. When we pretend to be mind readers, we only know what we think that other people think. We assume that they see us the same way we see ourselves. As you saw, this could be the exact opposite of what other people really think.

When I returned to my office I asked myself why I did not apply the same reasoning to Stanton? Why did I assume that I knew what Gary thought? Was I a mind reader? Maybe it was only the fear of rejection, which is present in all of us, that caused me to stop calling.

The next morning I called again. The secretary asked me: "May I ask who is calling?"

"Henry Ekstein." I answered.

"Let me see if he is available."

After a minute, she transferred me to her boss. Gary was very warm and friendly. He apologized that he had not called sooner, but that most of the time he had been out of the country. He told me that his number one problem was lack of time. He quoted Leonardo da Vinci, who had the same problem. I could tell that the man was also knowledgeable in areas other than business.

He told me that he had read the articles and was very impressed. He wanted me to give a management briefing to his executives on "Managing to Encourage change." I asked him if there was a specific problem that he wanted me to emphasize in my briefing. He answered that he would like me to stress the aspect of timely implementation of changes. He felt that by the time most managers decided to implement the needed changes, the conditions were no longer the same, and the changes needed were completely different. In other words, by the time changes are implemented they are usually already out of date.

He asked me to fax him a letter of agreement, and I faxed him a standard agreement right away. Within few minutes, he faxed me back the signed document. I was amazed at the speed with which the man made the decision. Maybe that was one reason why he had become the Chairman and CEO of a large corporation.

I also learned the following important lessons.

1. Do not try to guess what other people think. We are not mind readers.

2. Never give up. Persistence pays off.

3. Do not procrastinate. Make decisions quickly, and implement changes in a timely manner.

Chapter 17

The "Slotting" Principle

> Do not despise any man and do not consider anything as impossible; for there is not a man who has not his hour and there is not a thing that has not its place.
> — Talmud, <u>Ethics of the Fathers</u> Chapter IV, Mishnah 3

I recall a case of a very capable CFO who, in my opinion, had the ability to become the president of the company. When the incumbent president retired, the board of directors decided to look for a suitable replacement outside the company because they did not believe that any executive presently in the company could do the job.

This last point requires some explanation. Many executives tend to "slot" people. They put them into "slots" and believe that this is where they belong. "This is a clerk; he will probably be a poor office manager. This is an assembler; you cannot make him a supervisor."

When Truman became president of the United States, the media wondered how could a haberdasher run a country. They slotted him as a haberdasher. One newspaper printed a caricature showing a tiny Truman sitting in a big chair. Despite that, today most historians think that he was a good president.

This action, which I call "slotting" prevents many capable managers and employees from being promoted and robs companies of the benefits of using the talents of their employees to the fullest. We seem to forget that most great people started in low positions and worked their way up.

I asked the CFO why he would not ask the board of directors to appoint him as the next president of the company. He answered, "I may be able to do the job, however, the board of directors might be looking for somebody who is prominent in the industry has the experience as well as a good track record running a large company. As good as I am I do not meet the required qualifications."

"Neither did President Truman. He was a haberdasher." I said.

I pointed out that he, the CFO, had many advantages over outsiders. The directors had known him for many years. They knew that he was honest, he knew the company, he earned the respect of all managers and employees, had good knowledge of company products, was excellent in human relations, and easily evoked trust. He knew many of the important customers and would have a relatively short learning period. Most importantly, he was bright and open-minded and had, in my opinion, the ability to be an excellent president. I told him that I knew many presidents of companies and that he was better qualified for the job than ninety percent of them.

However, the CFO was hesitating. He said, "This is a great responsibility. All employees and their families depend on the company. Their livelihood depends on the success of the company."

I was amazed at his sense of responsibility. Most managers that I knew would have jumped at the opportunity to get promoted to the position of a president without thinking much of the great responsibility. They would have extolled their virtues, skills and abilities to do the job without a shred of humility. By contrast, here was a humble, decent man who put the interests of the company and the interests of employees before his own. This convinced me even more that he should be the president, and I decided that I must do everything possible to encourage him.

I told him that if he did not take this position someone else, less honest and probably less capable, would. He thought for a while and in the end agreed with me. I told him that I was confident that with his people skills and his presentation ability he would be able persuade the board of directors to make the right decision.

This convinced him. He went to the board of directors. I do not know what he told them but he must have done something right because he called me in the evening to tell me that he got the job.

He became an outstanding president. He increased sales of the company, through internal growth and through acquisitions, from fifty million dollars to almost one and a half billion dollars in ten years. He hired first-rate executives and offered them incentive plans tied to the growth of the company. He raised the morale of employees dramatically, and improved their benefit package. The stock soared from two to forty five dollars a share and the company is now considered as one of the fastest growing in the industry and perhaps in the United States.

The business community started paying attention to the company. Forbes magazine included it in its "buy list" of ten fast growing US companies. One industrial giant planned a hostile takeover of the company but did not succeed. The president was perceived as a leader in the industry. He became chairman of prestigious industrial associations. He was invited on many occasions to give speeches here and abroad, and to preside over ceremonies honoring VIPs for their contributions in various fields. Magazines wrote articles and cover stories about the president adding prestige to the man and to the company.

The president refuses to take credit for these impressive achievements. He always points out that he is surrounded by excellent executives and employees, who helped him grow the company, and that they deserve much of the credit.

The name of this former CFO and now Chairman, President and CEO of the company is Mark S. Newman. The name of the company is DRS Technologies.

I hate to think of what would have happened to the company if Mark were prevented from becoming a president because of slotting. In all probability the company its shareholders and its employees would not have achieved the success they enjoy today.

Another case illustrating the effects of slotting is the story of the founders of Apple Computer. Steve Jobs gives an account of what happened to him when he came to Hewlett-Packard and suggested the idea of a PC. They checked his records of education and said to him, "Hey, we don't need you. You have not gotten through college yet."

Slotting is so deeply ingrained in most people, that instead of judging the man and his ideas on their merits, Steve Jobs was slotted as a student or perhaps as a college dropout, whose ideas cannot be taken seriously. The idea of a PC was also slotted as something impossible and of no commercial value. Obviously, they were wrong on both scores. After that unpleasant experience Steve Jobs and Steve Wozniak founded Apple Computer. They followed William Swanson's rule: "Look for what is missing. Many know how to improve what is there; few can see what is not there."

These case studies taught me a great deal about lost opportunities that can be caused by slotting. If you, the reader, come across slotting in your company, make sure that it does not cripple the company's growth.

Chapter 18

The Big Rocks Principle

> Have fun in what you do. It will be reflected in your work. No one likes a grump except another grump!
>
> — *William H. Swanson, Chairman and CEO of Raytheon*

One day, my daughter sent me the following story, which she thought, would be of interest to me. I am including it here because it might be of interest to you, the reader, as well. Its author is unknown.

An expert in time management was speaking to a group of business students and, to drive home a point, used a compelling illustration.

As he stood in front of the group of high-powered overachievers he said, "Okay, time for a quiz," and he pulled out a one-gallon mason jar and set it on the table in front of him. He also produced about a dozen fist-sized rocks and carefully placed them, one at a time, into the jar. When the jar was filled to the top and no more rocks would fit inside, he asked, "Is this jar full?" Everyone in the class yelled, "Yes!"

The time management expert replied, "Really?" He reached under the table and pulled out a bucket of gravel. He dumped some gravel in and shook the jar causing the pieces of gravel to work themselves down into the spaces between the big rocks. He then asked the group once more, "Is the jar full?"'

By this time, the class was on to him. "Probably not." one of them answered.

"Good!" he replied. He reached under the table and got a bucket of sand. He poured sand in the jar until all of the spaces left between the rocks and the gravel were filled in. Once more, he asked the question, "Is this jar full?"

"No!" the class shouted. Once again, he said, "Good."

Then he took a pitcher of water and began to pour until the jar was filled to the brim. He looked at the class and asked, "What is the point of this illustration?"

One eager beaver said, "The point is, no matter how full your schedule is, if you try really hard you can always fit some more things in it!"

"No," the speaker replied, "That's not the point. The truth this illustration teaches us is, "If you don't put the big rocks in first, you'll never get them in at all. We need to discover what the big rocks in our lifetime are: loved ones, faith, education, your dreams, a worthy cause, friends, teaching or mentoring others? Remember to put the big rocks in first or you'll never get them in at all."

So, when you are reflecting on this short story, ask yourself this question: What are the big rocks in my life? Then, put those in your jar first.

Discovering what is important in life is easy for some people and difficult for others. Some people never discover what their big rocks are.

The same applies to business. However, in business those who do not discover what is important pay a high economic price: They go out of business and often lose their entire investment.

It is, therefore, crucial to define the important things in business, what needs to be done to increase profit, market share or whatever else that you want to achieve.

There are some executives who know the important things that need to be done in order to make their business grow and still fail because they do not have the initiative and drive to do something about it, or do not know how to allocate their time to each important issue. Many who know what needs to be done fail because they are afraid to make decisions, and implement the necessary changes. Others do the right things, but fail because they implement the necessary changes too late.

Timing is very important. If you produce umbrellas after the rainy season is over, you will have to carry them in inventory until the next season. If you do not have the capital to carry them in inventory, you may have to sell them below cost. Either way your profits will be wiped out.

The importance of allocation of time to important issues is sometimes overlooked. Time is a limited resource. We have a limited number of hours a day in which to work. Moreover, most important achievements, perhaps 70% or 80% of them, are usually accomplished in a small fraction of time available, perhaps 20% or 30% of it. The balance of time is spent on unimportant things. The 80/20 rule, also known as Pareto's law, is at work here as well. The 80/20 rule is so important in business and generally in life that we should explain it here briefly.

The economist and sociologist Vilfredo Pareto (1848-1923) analyzed about hundred years ago the distribution of wealth in England in the 19th century. He found that twenty percent of the population owned eighty percent of wealth. Pareto investigated different countries and different periods and found that this imbalance repeated itself.

The same imbalance existed in distribution of income. When comparing two sets of data, of population and of income, about 80% of income was earned by 20% of income earners. The 80/20 numbers are not etched in stone. In some cases, we may find the numbers to be 70/30. Nor do they have to total a hundred, because they are from two different sets of data, which cannot be added. You cannot add population to income just like you cannot add apples and pears. It therefore could happen, say, that fifteen percent of the population earns seventy percent of income. The important issue is that there is an imbalance. The relationship is not proportional.

You find a similar imbalance in many areas of business. Twenty percent of salesmen produce eighty percent of sales. Twenty percent of customers order eighty percent of merchandise. Look around and you will probably find many other examples of this rule. This rule is also important in time management.

Most managers have more things to do than time in which to do them. This is often due to flaws in work delegation and time allocation. To make the best use of your time, review your schedule periodically, perhaps every month or two. Start out by reviewing your schedule more often, maybe once a week. Evaluate each item on the schedule by asking the following questions:

a. Why is it important to do it?

b. Does it contribute to company sales?

c. Does it contribute to company profits?

d. Is it good for employees?

e. Does it produce other benefits?

If the answer to above questions is "no" or a weak "yes", ask yourself what would happen if you did not do it. If an item is of marginal importance, you should probably spend your time on more important things.

If the answer to one or more of the above questions is "yes" ask yourself if you can delegate the item to somebody else in the company whose time is less critical. However, make sure to follow up. When you delegate you are still responsible for results. You can only delegate the authority needed to perform the function but not the responsibility for doing it.

Ideally, you should delegate the item to the lowest level manager or employee who can still perform the function well. For example if the company needs to be represented in a regional industry meeting and your secretary, after receiving the invitation put it on your schedule, ask her to find out what level of executives will be participating in this meeting. If only lower level executives will be participating and you are the president, ask yourself if one of your vice presidents or department managers could go to this meeting. This is a good example of the type of items, which you could spend eighty percent of your time on, producing only marginal benefits.

In each case, ask yourself if the item is such that if you spent your time on it the results would be substantial. Examples of such items are a lunch with an important customer, meeting a CEO whose company you wish to acquire, a presentation to the board of directors, meeting important business or political leaders who can directly or indirectly help you increase sales and profits. For example, if you are in the defense business, such an important leader could be an admiral, a general or a senator who has influence over what the armed forces buy and from whom they buy it.

After deleting items that are not important, and delegating what you can to others, you have to schedule the important items, which you want to handle in person. When making your schedule keep in mind that delaying the handling of an item may cause it to be overlooked, because we do not know what new issues we will have to deal with next week.

George Buckley, Chairman and CEO of Brunswick Corporation, told me a story about Leonardo da Vinci. A student approached da Vinci who was busy painting a portrait. The student needed the master's help in solving a problem and asked him when he could spend some time with him. The master, who believed that helping students was important, said that he was seventy years old and that at his age the only time to schedule important things was now. In a way, we are all in the same boat because we do not know what will happen tomorrow.

Another problem is important items that we hate to deal with. Many managers tend to postpone dealing with these items until tomorrow, next week, or leave it for "some other time."

The result is that rather than dealing with the item once, they live through the agony of dealing with the hated item many times. Thus, if something you do not like to do must be done and you cannot delegate it to someone else, do it as soon as possible. Get it over with and proceed to other more pleasant issues.

When scheduling your work, be sure to allocate some time for business activities that you enjoy. Among these are playing golf with an important client, or discussing business problems with a consultant who gives you good advice, and whose company you enjoy. Disperse these items among less pleasant activities. This helps reduce tensions and gives you something to look forward to.

William H. Swanson of Raytheon sent me his refreshing booklet "(Un)written Rules of Management". On the first page he wrote to me: "Henry, Enjoy!" This summarizes an important principle in life. Swanson writes in his booklet "Have fun in what you do. We all spend many, many hours doing what we do. It is much more pleasant to spend those hours with people who have a bounce in their step and a smile on their face than with those who mistakenly associate professionalism with being sour and dour".

How true! Looking at some professionals you might think that they feel guilty if they enjoy a business activity. Observing them you might think that they feel that if they enjoy what they do they should not get a salary, but rather pay the company for the entertainment. In reality nothing is further from truth. To be successful a man must enjoy what he is doing. If he does it only for the money, his performance will be mediocre at best.

We can summarize this chapter as follows:

- Identify what is most important to you, the "big rocks".
- Allocate most of your time to these important items
- Delegate what you can and make sure to follow up.
- Disperse business activities you enjoy among less pleasurable tasks.
- Finally, do not feel guilty if business is fun. Enjoying your work is good for business.